Advance praise for

Peace and Pedagogy PRIMER

"Vivid, engaging, provocative, and profoundly touching, this book issues an imperative and timely call for re-imagining peace and pedagogies of peace through children's eyes, teachers' visions, and teacher educators' commitments. Multilayered and multidimensional, peace and pedagogical cultivation of inner peace and outer peace are envisioned as a daily practice, at the site of subjectivity and intersubjectivity, through images and words, to both curb violence and promote loving relationality. Filled with rare insights, inspirations, and wisdom, this is an essential and landmark book for every educator to answer the call for pedagogy of, about, and for peace. Open the book to be inspired."

—Hongyu Wang, Professor, Curriculum Studies,
Oklahoma State University-Tulsa;
Author of *Nonviolence and Education: Cross-Cultural Pathways*

"The *Peace and Pedagogy Primer* offers a rich contribution through its conceptually sophisticated analysis of the foundations of and debates in the field of peace education. Molly Quinn also offers unique perspectives on teacher education through the use of innovative visual methodologies to understand and promote peace in our classrooms and communities."

—Monisha Bajaj, Associate Professor,
International and Multicultural Education,
Director, Master of Arts in Human Rights Education,
University of San Francisco

Peace and Pedagogy PRIMER

This book is part of the Peter Lang Education list.
Every volume is peer reviewed and meets
the highest quality standards for content and production.

PETER LANG
New York • Washington, D.C./Baltimore • Bern
Frankfurt • Berlin • Brussels • Vienna • Oxford

Molly Quinn

Peace and Pedagogy PRIMER

PETER LANG
New York • Washington, D.C./Baltimore • Bern
Frankfurt • Berlin • Brussels • Vienna • Oxford

Library of Congress Cataloging-in-Publication Data
Quinn, Molly.
Peace and pedagogy primer / Molly Quinn.
pages cm. — (Peter Lang primers)
Includes bibliographical references and index.
1. Peace—Study and teaching. I. Title.
JZ5534.Q55   303.6'6071—dc23   2014002012
ISBN 978-1-4331-1844-9 (paperback)
ISBN 978-1-4539-1323-9 (e-book)

Bibliographic information published by **Die Deutsche Nationalbibliothek**.
Die Deutsche Nationalbibliothek lists this publication in the "Deutsche
Nationalbibliografie"; detailed bibliographic data are available
on the Internet at http://dnb.d-nb.de/.

Cover design by Clear Point Designs

The paper in this book meets the guidelines for permanence and durability
of the Committee on Production Guidelines for Book Longevity
of the Council of Library Resources.

*To the children of the world
and their teachers,
to all their dreams for peace*

Contents

Illustrations

Acknowledgments

I began this work challenged by the notion that peace must begin with me, in working from within. Through it, I was drawn further as well to the claim that to realize peace in our world we must begin with children, which took me also to engagement with those who would and do teach children. In reflecting on what I had discovered from and through and with them all, I concluded here with the profound and abiding call of personhood, realized ever in relationship, in the transformation of relationship, in transformative relationship. As in the Ubuntu tradition, beseeching us ever to take up the challenge to be and to become fully human, I was reminded that a person is indeed a person through others.

There are so many others through whom I have found and sought to cultivate and continue to pursue my own personhood—too many truly to name—through this project. Yet, among the many "peacemakers" who have succored me in manifold, varied and nearly infinite ways, I want to specifically acknowledge: Emily Smith, Molly Cutler, Callie Heilmann, Lauren Perovich and Eunice Yun for invaluable research assistance; Jai Jackson, my angel of technology; and all those at Peter Lang who have labored much and most patiently on my behalf—Sophie Appel, Phyllis Korper, Stephen Mazur and Chris Myers. I also cannot thank Shirley Steinberg enough for the honor of inclusion in this Primer series, and much besides. I have been the recipient of unspeakable support, as well, in the completion of this work from Petra Hendry, Ann Trousdale, Kenny Varner, Marianne Frye and Steve Triche. I am most grateful, too, for the inspiring scholarship and feedback of Dale Snauwaert, Monisha Bajaj and Hongyu Wang concerning the pursuit of peace, justice and nonviolence.

Originally planning to limit my inquiries into peace and possibilities of teaching for peace to my photography project studies with pre-service teachers in my social studies education courses, I am especially indebted to Debbie Sonu—inspired, tireless, brilliant and soulful colleague and friend—who through her own work and hospitality in recruiting me to it gave me the opportunity to carry this study forward into classrooms with teachers and children. She has also been an ever-present source of insight, inspiration and encouragement. And, this inquiry and the insights, questions and directions issuing from it would not have been possible without all the aspiring teachers, practicing teachers and children with whom I worked, and their generosity in offering their participation, experience, thought and reflection to such study. Though they must here remain unnamed, in their very persons in both their visions and voices they saturate this text.

Chapter 1
Picturing Peace: A Beginning

Many of us worry about the situation of the world. We don't know when the bombs will explode.... As individuals, we feel helpless, despairing. The situation is so dangerous, injustice is so widespread.... if we panic, things will only become worse. But if even one person...can remain calm, lucid, knowing what to do and what not to do,.... one such person can save the lives of many.

Our world is something like a small boat. Compared with the cosmos, our planet is a very small boat. We are about to panic because our situation is no better than the situation of the small boat on the [stormy] sea. You know that we have more than 50,000 nuclear weapons. Humankind has become a very dangerous species. We need people who can sit still and be able to smile, who can walk peacefully. We need people like that in order to save us.... You are that person...each of you is that person.

Thich Nhat Hanh (1987/1996, pp. 11–12)

Beginning with Me:
Problem-Posing [1] for Pedagogical Studies in Peace

"Let there be peace on earth and let it begin with me..." The words never rang out so boldly or movingly as when my Uncle Harley, in his gorgeous baritone voice, sang them for us when our families gathered each Christmas. Though it has been some time since his passing, every year I miss him more, and this event and inspiration especially, during the holiday season. And while I sit now at a café in Cold Spring, New York—far from home and childhood, the day after Thanksgiving, writing to the sounds of Christmas music, these memories envelop me; and my quests for and queries into peace, the

---

1 The idea of problem-posing comes from the work of Paulo Freire (1970/1993) as at the heart of the pedagogical project—"the posing of the problems of human beings in their relations with the world" (p. 60), through which "people develop their power to perceive critically the way they exist in the world..." (p. 64). Herein, education affirms the subjectivity of teachers and students, as unfinished beings in the process of becoming, with the capacity to come together—in thought and dialogue and action—to transcend themselves and transform the world.

possibilities of educating for peace, cannot be severed from such bittersweet remembrances. Even in this, too, I am caught up with the ironies and contradictions: Christmas, consumerism, and capitalism; Christo-centric histories and legacies across the world marred by and mired in oppression and violence.

> Peace—prayerful, powerful presence and freely practiced
>   praxis[2] of fellowship;
> Embracing engagement, experience, and existence with
>   equanimity, joy, and
> Awe, awakeness, appreciation—even in the face of suffering
>   or wrong;
> Cultivating communion, community, compassion; countering
>   hatred, injustice, to
> Enter ever into relation, whole and wholly, humbly,
>   hospitably, unconditionally encountering all in truth,
>   … and in the generous—forgiving?—beauty of peace:
> Ah yes! A love most radical[3] indeed.

I scribble a word play on peace, trying to get to the heart of my heart for peace—this personal, professional, and beyond, preoccupation and occupation for such a long time now, it seems, I can scarcely imagine a time when peace didn't seek a place in my mind or movement, or I in its sweet abode and company.[4] In this way, I am com-

---

2 Freire (1970/1993) also grounds his work in the notion of praxis, in which the centrality of reflection, thought, and responsiveness are highlighted in any lived practice and are at the heart of any truly affirmative and transformative human action.

3 The work of critical pedagogy, specifically as articulated by Freire (1970/1993), issues from what he calls "radical love"; reflected here in my thinking about peace, which has love—for life, the world, humanity—at its roots, without which no dialogue or communion or collective project is truly possible. Joe Kincheloe (2004) defines this term of Freire's in relation to a "guiding light," along with justice and respect, by which all things become possible as we work together in solidarity. Herein heart and mind are linked in labor "to increase our capacity to love, to bring the power of love into our everyday lives and institutions, and to rethink reason in a humane and interconnected manner" (p. 3).

4 I recently came across a quote somewhere by Kathleen Norris (1931) that read "Peace—that was the other name for home" (p. 155). For some time interested in and inquiring into hospitality and the appreciable intellectual work undertaken around it, some respecting education—curriculum and pedagogy (See Quinn, 2009), I wanted

pelled to begin with "me"—myself, as it were, indeed—in contemplating peace on earth, though peace ever seems to both elude and allure me. For in just these brief musings, peace finds affiliation with other all-encompassing ideals—and as difficult to understand much less stand in and for—like justice, love, and liberation. I also paradoxically cling to the language of religion herein, perhaps to counter that of scientism, instrumentalism, objectivism, functionalism, business, management—discourses dominating so much of our understandings of and standings in relation to education, pedagogical thought and practice, and policy.

I/Eye on Peace & Subjectivity: Want of Peace, Wanting Peace, Want of Wanting Peace

I affirm subjective experience, the quintessentially human—such immeasurable, beyond measure, intangibilities, and irreplaceable singularities yet experiential, discernible palpabilities and profundities of priority—as lived of the heart and mind and spirit. For the normative paradigm rooted in science and industry bears its share in oppression and violence as well. Others might find reference to the language of the aesthetic, poetic, humanities, more comfortable than that of religion, and in complementing possibly rather than countering, that of the scientific, techno-rational, executive managerial. Perhaps, in this embrace—however problematic for the sanctity of the secular in the academy (Wexler, 2000, 2002), and separation of church and state—I seek greater inclusion of and dialogue among a multiplicity of visions and voices herein.

I unabashedly, begin, though, too, as I undertake this inquiry with the discomfiting, or perhaps many discomfitings, concerning the meanings and makings of peace, and aspirations for such educationally, pedagogically, including my not-without-difficulty-or-controversy assumption and assertion, that education can and ought

---

here to call attention to a possible affiliation among such concepts and ideas—peace, home, hospitality; and suggest that particularly in an era of marked globalization and transmigration, perhaps so much literature featuring home and homelessness implicitly entails a search for peace as well (See Quinn, 2011).

to address the question and cause of peace, and even have such principally in view. Such is really neither new nor "radical," rooted in educational traditions dating back to antiquity as in Seneca's notion of cultivating our humanity (Nussbaum, 1997) and Socrates' interests in self-knowledge, truth, and the good (Plato, ca. 380 BC/1992); as well as those too of such visionary world teachers as Confucius, Moses, Mohammad, Jesus, and the Buddha—each in his own way a messenger of the wisdom and way of peace. My inquiries have indeed led me to the inspirations of these and other more contemporary global leaders (for example, Gandhi, King, Mother Teresa, the Dalai Lama), as well as anew to the work of Paulo Freire (1970/1993) and his educational call to "the vocation of humanization" in a world yet alarmingly defined by violence, oppression, dehumanization, and manifold injustice. Through such, constitutive of peace is a certain criticality[5] and praxis of "radical love" (See footnote 3). Without detouring to genealogical tracings of such traditions except to highlight recent renewed interests in and critical analyses of the (im)possibilities[6] of education as a project aimed at justice[7] or emancipation (Ranciere, 1991; den Heyer, 2009; Biesta, 2010), I do wish here to set before us a key consideration: criticality, praxis, radical love and the pursuit of peace must engage not just or perhaps even principally the language of ethics—which is the path to it most taken up in the educational realm—but also the language of desire.

This distinction was brought home to me most convincingly recently through a study on women and violence of the Centre for Research on Theories and Practices for Overcoming Inequalities (CREA) at the University of Barcelona, presented by researcher Lidia Puigvert (2010): youth, particularly young women, revealed what she called a "dis-integration of meaning" (in concert with Weber's analy-

---

5 For more on the import of the critical in relation to peace education, see Reardon and Snauwaert (2011), and the special issue of Bajaj (2008).

6 I use here (im)possibilities to denote particularly poststructuralist renderings of the mutually constitutive aspects of that deemed possible or impossible, as well as more specifically here to highlight the questions recent scholarship has raised concerning the actual possibility or even desirability of emancipatory goals for and approaches to education.

7 For more on some of the critiques raised against social justice as an educational aim, see Quinn et al., 2013.

sis of the crisis of modernity) concerning romantic love and sexual attraction and committed relationship—though each knew it was preferred to desire the good, and even suspected that he or she would eventually commit to and settle down with a partner who was good, in concert with the language of ethics; the language of desire most entertained reflected a predominant passion for the "bad" boy or girl, passion and allure allied with the dominating, abusive, and even violent. Reflecting certain hetero-normativity respecting romance, relationship, and desire, males in the study reported the pressure to be or become "bad" or perform "badness" in order to even be deemed desirable to young women as well. "Gangsta glam," "urban youth porn"—violence is sexy, still, it seems. And the language of ethics and the language of desire seem also to be in some serious conflict—the good and beautiful at odds.

Promoting Peace Pedagogically? | Politics, Plurality, and the Presence of Tension

Such an articulation does not exactly elucidate some of my own discomfitings here, though—or maybe such does. I find myself uneasy in taking up the explicitly political, respecting education, as well as any singular or particular agenda—the call of peace certainly is in some ways necessarily political—integrally tied to questions of justice, equity, power, freedom, and subject at least to specificity of agenda, and the dangers of such, including the domination of some agenda to the exclusion of alternative, creative, renewing, collective, and ongoing interpretations of it, as well as other important perspectives, projects, and possibilities; and openness of inquiry too (Horowitz, 2009, April; 2009). This uneasiness dwells with an acknowledgement of the equally important assertions of scholars highlighting the inherently political nature of education as a social project, of curriculum, and of any knowledge system or claim (for example, Apple, 2004, 2006; Lather, 2007); and that the pursuit of objectivity is at least as elusive as it may be alluring. Indeed, as a matter of ethics, then, I proceed in a certain cautionary way—making a distinction and recognizing a difference between the inherently political and the explicitly politicized, intention and imposition, influence and indoctrination, education and propaganda, ideological conviction and ideological certainty.

In this, I have been influenced by Hannah Arendt (1954/1993), who in her essay on "The Crisis in Education" advocates a certain conservatism respecting education—perhaps including even for the sake of the political, creating a space apart from it; her call: "to cherish and protect something—the child against the world, the world against the child...; for the sake of what is new and revolutionary in every child, education...must preserve this newness and introduce it into an old world..." (pp. 192–193). This claim issues from her assertion not only that the world is "ever out of joint," requiring protection from our wear as well as ongoing renewal to persist, but also relatedly, that the essence of education is *natality*, the fact that new beings perpetually are born into the world—these, our responsibility, and our hope, testifying to our human capacity to begin again, to set things right, through such; which includes as well our capacity to imagine that which is possible in relation to setting the world right; herein, too, articulating the ontological root of human agency, and freedom—a "vocation of humanization" (Freire, 1970/1993) indeed.

We ought to acknowledge, in this way, perhaps, that education, too, is ever in crisis, like the world—ever out of joint; and, following Arendt's thought (1954/1993), our responsibility for its ongoing renewal, as well:

> Education is at the point at which we decide whether we love the world enough to assume responsibility for it and...save it from that ruin which, except for renewal, except for the coming of the new..., would be inevitable. And education...is where we decide whether we love our children enough not to expel them from our world and leave them to their own devices, nor to strike from their hands their chance of undertaking something new, something unforeseen by us, but to prepare them in advance for the task of renewing a common world. (p. 196)

Education, thus, may also be at the point at which, and where, we seek and find some integration of meaning, where matters of truth and goodness and beauty meet; at which matters of necessity, desire, and ethics all and each and together call for our response.

Herein is, at least in some measure, where desire encounters and perhaps also competes with—or engages not without some tensions—the ethical claim here, for me. In taking up this responsibility, and out of jointness, we also must reckon with—even as an act of love and attention to "that ruin" and that which ruins—the political, the implicatedness of education as "a technology of colonist subjectifica-tion," as postcolonial scholar Nina Asher (2009) puts it; the ways in which education, as a matter of fact as well as historical legacy, worked against the causes of justice and peace and love. Hongyu Wang (2010), positing the violence endemic to our educational institutions, seeks to articulate pedagogies of nonviolence. Responsi-ble and responsive education, then, seems to call for some kind of redress of this order, for counter-curriculum efforts at, of, and for love, peace, justice—ever accompanied by a commitment to the task of renewing a common world, including a renewal of our very ideas and imaginings concerning peace and nonviolence: what such might actually mean and require of us; even apart from pedagogy, politics, practice, and for their sake as well as our own, and for the new, yet to come, in our midst, who bring that which we do not and cannot to this endeavor.

In an educational context presently and in a heightened way dom-inated by what some have called an "audit culture," marked by mechanisms of surveillance and regulation—curriculum increasingly constituted by knowledge as framed through testing and standardiza-tion—which in truth serves to diminish thought, deny human desire, and detract from the question of ethics (Pinar, 2004; Taubman, 2009); respecting the work of education, Maxine Greene (2008) critically reminds us to ask: Accountable for what? And to whom? She brings us back to our responsibility—for the world's renewal; to the new among us, ever born alas it seems into a world marred by indifference and violence. To this task, I suggest, we need to bring all our capaci-ties, ideas, questions, languages, resources, our all, dialogically and pedagogically, together in conversation, toward imagining possibili-ties and praxes for peace in mending a broken world, and tending a vulnerable humanity. "Let there be peace on earth, and let it begin with me...." Beginning with me, beginning with you, beginning with us; imagine all the people, together...

Beginning with Children, through Those Who Teach Them: Toward Picturing Peace Pedagogically

Thus, I proceed with something of the heart of my project here, inquiring with faith, affirming that radical love, peace, justice, involves radical questioning and critique and listening; requires of us a living and laboring within the struggle and quest for such, and that we seek to engage our *desires* for peace as much as the ethical demands it entails embracing truth and necessity. Through this project, I seek to explore the work of education—curriculum and pedagogy specifically—with respect to the dream of peace, here particularly as issuing from the subjective gleanings of education students, prospective teachers, concerning their diverse ideas and experiences of peace. I seek to theorize—to rethink and re-imagine—peace, conceptually and pedagogically, through an analysis of the images students I have taught in my elementary and middle-grades social studies courses in New York City have collected and documented photographically to represent peace, and their reflections on them about what peace and teaching for peace might mean. Herein, I excavate something, I hope, of their imaginations and imaginings of and desires for peace—both personally and professionally, as well as their understandings regarding nonviolence as it relates to their work as aspiring teachers, here of social studies, to children. Inspired by Mohandas Gandhi's (1958) assertion that if we really want peace in the world, we must begin with children, herein I begin with those with whom I work who seek to teach children. For if, as it is written, "the hand that rocks the cradle is the hand that rules the world," the heart that teaches the child peace may be the hand that brings peace to the world, and the hope that heals the world by peace, as well.

In proceeding thus, in Chapter 2, I seek to first address the question: "Why 'Picturing Peace'?" In this way—the emphasis here on *picturing*—I hope to ground this work in a contemporary context in which the image is increasingly pervasive and dominant, a cultural multimedia milieu in which we are visually saturated and wherein our very ways of being, knowing, and learning are ever more and more inextricably tied up in what we "see." Relatedly, I posit for consideration the primacy of the imagination—that is, our visions of life, education, peace—in human understanding and activity, and thus a need to examine our own imaginings in relation to concerns and causes of human import, such as peace and educating for peace: our very picturing as precursors to our purposes and praxes in the world, such relates to the necessity and labor of re-picturing, re-imagining, together and in an ongoing way as well. Herein, I also present the path I have taken to discern and depict the vision and voice of the aspiring teachers with whom I have worked regarding the dream of peace and realizing it via pedagogy; outlining the parameters and limitations of such, my research, and delineating the perspectives I bring to it, in addition to the pedagogical and methodological practices constitutive of it.

I turn in Chapter 3—"On Re-Imagining Peace, in Portraiture"—to the images and photographs of peace of my education students and aspiring teachers, and their significations of them. Here, through such, I seek to present a kind of portraiture of peace that is thematically representative of their imaginings and re-imaginings, as drawn from their own lives and experiences. I do so, based on this analysis, through the frames of nature, people, animals, peace places and objects, symbols of peace, and peace's opposites and singularities. The roles of memory and relationship emerge as important facets to any lived conceptions of peace, which propel us at the chapter's end toward further conceptualizing and defining prospective teachers' understandings of peace issuing from these images.

Thus, Chapter 4, "A Word Worth a Thousand Pictures," works to cohesively articulate and conceptually elucidate the meanings made by and taken from these education students respecting peace, as gleaned in their reflective writings upon peace and "picturing" peace via the experiences and outcomes of their photographic journeys and documentations. Engaging such images and the meanings attached to them in relation to certain pictorial, symbolic, and etymological histories of peace, I attempt to set forth these prospective teachers' conceptions of peace as experienced, and as constituted in the unique experience of "being" itself, in time. Further, in exploring their work, peace emerges not only as consciously experienced experience, but is also described as affirmative and desirable, marked by a sense of unity—what I call "with-ness" (that is, akin to harmony, integration, communion), and summons one to an ethics of responsibility amid much that is at odds with peace in this world. While presenting these shared findings, the chapter concludes with an eye to the "Eye/I" of inquiry, the singular and subjective source of peace, and pedagogy, as conceived, and lived.

From the understandings of peace made and made manifest by these education students, Chapter 5—"On the Way of/to Peace"— turns to a discussion of the pedagogical implications and possibilities they take up in reflecting upon such meanings as prospective teachers. This exploration is framed through an emphasis on the teacher as an active and intentional "peacemaker": embracing and embodying peace personally and professionally, engaging community as curriculum and endorsing therein a person-centered pedagogy, and explicitly educating for peace and enacting peace practices in the classroom. The chapter concludes with a brief reflection on two lived examples in the case of former education students, now teachers—respecting a peace curriculum in a first-grade class, and an inquiry into violence in a fourth-grade class, who offered me the opportunity to visit them in their classrooms, observe their work and speak with them about peace and violence, and their design of curriculum and pedagogy for addressing such.

Having had the privilege of visiting these two classrooms of three former students (two co-teaching in the first-grade classroom), and the opportunity to conduct visits in two additional elementary school classrooms in New York City, in Chapter 6, "Seeking Peace through Children's Eyes," I present a small glimpse into children's views on peace and education for peace, based on my initial efforts to "picture peace" with them—using literature, storytelling, and drawing, as well as photography—through focus-group activities and discussions, and individual interviews. In having worked here with roughly four students at each school—albeit also principally with those in the two schools and classrooms of former students, their portraits of peace are considered in relation to the peace possibilities elucidated by the (prospective) teachers in my study as well.

Finally, in "On Re-Imagining Peace and Pedagogies for Peace," I seek to share what I have gleaned from these engagements and explorations: possibilities that might make for more vitalizing portraits of peace and pedagogies for peace among us—animated by and inclusive of ethics and desire; for picturing peace heroically, for pursuing a treasured humanity on earth. This concluding chapter—inspired, no doubt, by my own desires to integrate, synthesize, crystallize, the fruits of my inquiry, and to ethically propel myself forward—brings me back, in a sense, to my own subjectivity, and the meanings and makings of peace issuing from such. Drawing upon connections made to existing literature, seeking that which is at the heart of my findings, encountering new questions, I begin again with me, summoning myself first to this journey, to engage afresh my own passion for peace and praxis of peace, in hopes that others too shall take up each in their own ways the call. Beginning with me, beginning with you, beginning with us; imagine all the people, together: peace on earth.

Chapter 2
Why "Picturing Peace"?

Every great advance...has issued from a new audacity of imagination.
-John Dewey (cited in Westbrook, 1991, p. 440)

The possible's slow fuse is lit by the imagination.
-Emily Dickinson (cited in Donoghue, 1984, p. 104)

Your imagination, my dear fellow, is worth more than you imagine.
-Louis Aragon (cited in Forencich, 2009, p. 161)

On Purpose, Passion, and the Power of Imagination

Imagine all the people living life in peace. You may say I'm a dreamer, but I'm not the only one. I hope someday you'll join us, and the world will live as one.   -John Lennon (1971)

Imagine all the people, the world living as one. John Lennon, artist and activist icon, here seems to express a profound desire for and heroic dream of peace, and a deep love of and responsibility to the world. Arendt (1954/1993), in articulating the essence of education as issuing from natality, speaks also of its referentiality: each of us, every child, is born into some community of others, into a people; into a world, and also for the sake of and toward the world, in love to the world—*amor mundi*—as well. She speaks, with her mentor Karl Jaspers, of the communion—*living as one*—necessary for the emergence of new life, for anything to come into being, and of our communicative passion for the world. From a study of her work, Patricia Bowen-Moore (1989) explicates her thought further in this way:

The child itself, then, is a worldly event whose birth signifies the reunion of lovers with the world and the world with them. (p. 17)

Thus, natality is disclosed as an entirely world-oriented (that is world-ly) phenomenon whose capacity for beginning anew ideally is for the sake of the durability and futurity of the world we hold in common. (p. 2)

Education—despite itself, grounded in heart, hope and desire—
then, too, is a work of love, to and for the world, the child, and all the
people; a work also largely directed by the imagination: that is, how
the child is conceived, people envisioned, world dreamed. John
Lennon also both affirms and attests to the power of human imagination, its central place—incited—in initiating social change, transfor-
mations of which we can and must only first dream. Moreover, his
vision is expansive and ambitious—seeking to embrace a whole
world of immense diversity. One could argue that in some deep
sense, he too, in this, is an educator and curriculum worker.

Others who are more intimately involved with educational theory
and curriculum thought have asserted the primacy, largely uncon-
scious, of the imagination, and the ways the images and ideas we
hold—about life, world, self, other, community, culture, peace,
justice, education, schooling—direct thought, belief, language, and
practice, and this in ways that all too often go unrecognized and
unquestioned (for examples, see Huebner, 1999; Greene, 1995/2000;
Eisner, 1979/2001; Apple, 2004, 2006; Gaudelli, 2011). This oversight
is, alas, perhaps overlooked most profoundly in dominant public
conceptions and expressions of curriculum, teaching, and schooling,
as well. Addressing educational concerns for citizenship in a global
context in which the image dominates, and is increasingly sanctified,
Bill Gaudelli (2011)—as he seeks to re-inhabit seeing, re-view its
habits, and draw attention to its totalizing and naturalizing gaze—
asks us to imagine a "pedagogy of seeing" *with* rather than *at*. Such
entails re-viewing what is yet unseen in what we see; "deep seeing,"
exploring what we can see beyond seeing; faithfully attending to our
very own ·seeing in and of the world, each other, and ourselves.
Herein, too, he seems to offer me doubled pedagogical and research
reasoning for undertaking this work. Much of what we think we
know and do is so powerfully tied to what we see, or imagine we see,
and make of such seeing.

Implicit here then is a call to educate our imaginations, or to perhaps first educate ourselves about our own imaginations, implicated
in both the language of desire and that of ethics we take up. If we
were to hope for, imagine, "all the people living life in peace," and
consider the curricular possibilities of educating for such a hope,

though, we must ask ourselves: What dreams and images and ideas of peace actually inform such an aspiration? What diversity of dreams, images, ideas, and aspirations intersect with the call for peace? And what of those at work to silence this call or obscure this vision?[1] This project, in some small, new, and embryonic way, hopes to take such up for examination.

Yet, despite Lennon, most of our discourses on peace seem to lack the element of the heroic, perhaps even existing apart from strong desire. Certainly, inquiring into "peace" does not have a daring, valiant, epic quality of appeal, nor is it esteemed or edgy in the way that examining justice or freedom—or injustice or oppression, for instance, might be: peace, in fact, may conjure images of new-age airheads, nuevo-hippies, soft-hearted and -headed liberals, or beauty pageant queen advocates on cue. Critique may come as well concerning the erasure of difference, endorsement of homogeneity, and establishment of harmony—a hegemonic peace—that is normatively feigned. Yet, Martin Luther King, Jr. (cited in Carson, 2000, p. 170), another revered public icon, actually posits genuine peace to be, rather than the absence of tension, the presence of justice itself.[2] And, peace is also certainly the cry heard around the world in present times—politically, personally, professionally (and we might add also

---

1 I do not here personally wish to privilege sight, per se, nor unwittingly support an ableism that presently already educationally marginalizes so many. I would suggest that "vision"—as pertaining to the imagination and the ways in which we hold and approach life and dream the future, albeit experienced and articulated in many different ways—is something somehow implicit in and integral to human life. Additionally, in a global scene in which the image is increasingly dominant, my engagement with students respecting images (via photography) here is not only for convenience, if you will, in order to get at student ideas about peace, but is also for a certain pedagogical timeliness and relevance as well.

2 In his book on *The Just*, the philosopher Paul Ricoeur (1995/2000) relatedly asserts this relation in asking: "Is peace not also the ultimate horizon of politics thought of as a cosmo-politic?" (p. x); and articulating that justice via the law seeks to make for social peace in addressing injustice, and violence.

economically)—in so many ways, and for good reason.[3] In league
with these "progressives," the educational philosopher John Dewey
(1957, p. 115) makes the claim that the only way to end war is to make
peace heroic. In a time of such heightened concerns for peace—
however defined, and oft in contrast to and remedy for experience as
lived, contemporary existence[4]—education may be at the point where
desire and ethics can finally meet to indeed make peace heroic. Such a
task involves not only imagining, but then re-imagining peace as well.
This work requires, via generative imaginings, inquiring into a
diversity of thought and practice, toward uncovering diverse possibilities for peace wherein difference and solidarity may be engaged and
affirmed, and power reckoned with—and perhaps "differently," for
peace. For Dewey, too, this kind of path of social reform is in fact best
found upon the path of education itself.

    With respect to addressing such a task, Maria Montessori (in
McCarthy, 2001, p. 35)—having influenced markedly the work of
early childhood educators—concurs that cultivating peace is the work
of education (for her, politics can only keep us from war.). As a
visionary world teacher himself, Gandhi (1958) not only says that if
we would have peace, we must begin with the children, but also that
there is no way to peace—rather, peace itself is the way. His ideas
greet those of many such others here, too, in contemporary thought
and teaching (for example, the Dalai Lama, cited in Mehrotra, 2005;
Dalai Lama, 2007; Hanh, 1999), who suggest that peace must, yes,
begin with "me"—the self, the person, with the human subject: that
peace must be birthed from within each of us, aspired to as the way
by each of us. This is perhaps pivotal to our very "vocation of human-

---

3 One need only call to mind troubling situations in the Middle East, Libya, and
Japan, or the continuing recovery struggles in Haiti, and along the U.S. Gulf Coast in
the aftermath of the BP oil spill and recent hurricanes—as well as present fall-out
caused by tornadoes across the country, to get but a small sense of some of the critical
want of and need for peace worldwide. The rise in school violence, of children
perpetuating violence against children—such recent shocking and impactful
tragedies like that in an elementary school in Newtown, Connecticut, among them—
intensifies this cry for peace too.
4 Via such "subjective" definition, increasing and unanticipated dislocations (Asher,
2009) via globalization and feelings of "accelerated acceleration" (Hansen, 2008) have
been noted, for example.

ization" and also a matter of *conscientization*: the educational task of becoming keenly aware of our own biographic, existential situation concerning peace, such that we may transformatively act from such awareness (Freire, 1970/1993). Inspired by such provocations and possibilities, in seeking to attend to, through, and beyond myself to such a labor—this imagining and re-imagining, together and in relation to education, to children, and to peace as the way—I turn now to teachers and aspiring teachers of children—my students, prospective educators, inviting them to explore their own dreams of peace and ways to peace, and the curricular and pedagogical implications—perhaps varied and sundry, diverse and divergent—issuing from such study.

Frames on, Frame-"works" for Picturing Peace: A Peace Pursuit Project Portrait

Herein, admittedly, I continue beginning with me, from the textures of my lived experience and pedagogical engagement with my students, and through this project have compelled each student to begin with him- or herself as well. Thus, as I relate the frames, the frame-"works" through which I have sought to picture peace, understand education-student/prospective-teacher portraits of peace, and through such begin to re-imagine generative dreams of peace for our children and for us all via education, I foreground this description with my intention to eschew with Freire and his critique of the banking model of education—a model that in emphasizing knowledge transfer and transmission tends to deny the human, the human creativity and relationship at the heart of any genuine act of knowing, knowledge production, or presentation—a banking approach to research, to qualitative or curriculum inquiry, as well. By this, I mean here to acknowledge the dialogic manner in which I have approached this study (and hope, too, shall my reader, inquiring anew into his or her own dream of peace and responsibility respecting such in conversation with that which is set forth herein), engaging my own subjectivity in the study's design, analysis, and interpretation, in conversation with the subjectivities of my students, here specifically through their reflections on their experiences of and aspirations for peace as initiated through photography.

Necessarily, and ideally—in affirmation of natality, our responsibility and capacity to begin ever again for the renewal of the world via education and thus of education too—such has meant an emergent design, much unfolding in the course of open-ended inquiry and analysis. I liken such to Dewey's dedication to experimentation and depiction of research as "seek and ye shall find," see what you shall find; or to an inter-subjective experiment of and experience inspired by Pinar's method of *currere* (2004), one oriented toward uncovering and re-creating our own understandings and visions of peace in relation to our lived experiences, dialogically together. I liken such, perhaps, too, to an experiment akin to Gaudelli's call for a pedagogy of seeing (2011), an effort toward deep seeing, to inhabit our own seeing to see what we see and tend to fail to see—at least this is what I hoped for my students and hoped to find in study of their works on "picturing peace." Inspired by David Hansen (2011) to "begin with me," I intentionally sought to encourage myself, and my students, to embrace also the naïve "beginners mind" in undertaking this inquiry: to look anew at and into peace, for myself, for each self, in as open and fresh, natal, a way as possible. Here I was also influenced by the "play" of post-structuralism, which is also why I did not begin with the field of peace education, its literature, and appreciable contributions to our quest for peace, and that also educationally.[5]

---

5 Criticism of my study may be made respecting a certain theoretical and methodological eclecticism here. In this, I hope to affirm the constitutive and undeniable work of subjectivity at the heart of any research endeavor. As such, then, any effort at understanding, and of inquiry, is undertaken in and through one's biographic situation, life context, and process of living, necessitating a kind of acknowledgement of, reckoning with, integration of, and meaning-making with the ethics, desires, influences, questions, directions, etc., emerging from this scene of subjectivity. Admittedly, I have drawn upon and sought to make somewhat explicit what was brought to bear in this work here from my own life—perhaps which in itself in some ways affirms the pragmatism and process philosophy of Dewey, phenomenological and existentialist influence in Arendt's thought, the praxis of Freire central to critical pedagogy and the critical tradition, and the radical questioning of knowledge and subjectivity at the heart of poststructuralism and the postcritical traditions. All of these influences, despite and perhaps because of their differences and contradictions, contribute to my own work and understanding, and thus are brought together, for

And so I begin again with my own elementary and middle-school multicultural social-studies classes with prospective teachers in New York City, collecting their images of and reflections on peace over the past five years.[6] While a majority of these students reflect the national trend of those who enter the profession of teaching as White females in their twenties—here also academically privileged and of middle- to upper-middle class origins—some males, students of color, those from working-class backgrounds and career-changers beyond their twenties are also found among them, and in greater numbers than might be found in many other teacher education programs. Application to, admittance into, and enrollment in a program in an urban setting (and a city with one of the most diverse populations in the world) designed to prepare teachers to work in urban schools serving diverse populations of differing abilities and academic and social needs—one that strongly endorses a vision of inclusion and equity in education—may factor into this more diverse constitution, as well as suggest a number of shared commitments, possibly even related to aspirations toward teaching for social justice and peace.[7] Students are

---

better or worse, in this work. I have also been influenced here, methodologically speaking, by: Scheurich (1997/2001), toward postmodern inquiry that is dialogical; Lather (2007), in foregrounding not knowing and the limits of knowledge; Gunaratnam (2007), in embracing art forms as sources for broadening understanding in research; Pailliotet (1998), on deep viewing as critical method; and Werner (2004), on reading intertextuality in interpreting and interpretations of visual images.

6 It is only in the past five years, during my tenure at this university, that I have formally engaged this work with students, and collected their work issuing from such, as well: three classes, taught spring semesters 2006–2008, averaging 20 students per class (Clearly, I have not consistently taught the course every year, although I did also teach it in the summer of 2007 and fall of 2010. Due to the shortened course duration and corresponding syllabus adjustment for the summer course, student work in it is not included in this study; additionally, as data analysis was undertaken while I was still teaching the fall 2010 course, student work herein, as yet to be completed at the time, is also not included here.). While no students disqualified their work for such study, each class fell marginally short of a 100% yield, attributable to a student ending the term with an incomplete or dropping the class unexpectedly, or glitch in communications emailing photographs and such.

7 Such program enrollment also affords access to a great deal of background information about these students, autobiographically as well as demographically. For my purposes here, I have not drawn upon such information, except as grounded in my own knowledge of and experience with students—which is in many cases

also required to take this course; though while now at the beginning of their pre-service graduate work, some included in this study could at the time elect to take it at any time during their course of study, although they were encouraged to take it in their first semesters.

The students undertook this inquiry in each of my social studies classes through a course "pedagogical play" assignment[8] summarized in the following passage:

"Picturing Peace"

> Envision peace—and think and rethink it—with a disposable or digital camera, taking shots from your lived experience, in the course of your daily activities, that shed light on the way of peace—calling for or expressing such. Bring copies of your photos to class, with a 1- to 2-page reflection on the experience—analysis of the choices you made, the themes and questions emerging, the directions suggested via them for the work of peace, especially as a teacher (of social studies).

As students lived with this inquiry over the course of a month or so,[9] additional questions were posed through this project, such as:

---

appreciable, albeit for some more than others—as their teacher, and in continued relationship through their one- to two-year course of study in our program, participation in it as alumni, and enduring colleagueship. Such presents, no doubt, both limitations and possibilities, then, for the substance and scope of this study.

8 The syllabus introduces this course requirement in this way: "Throughout the semester, most class meetings require 'Pedagogical Play' responses to the readings and activities engaged in class. While many of these responses are autobiographically analytical, others are 'aesthetically' oriented—requiring artistic and/or performative in-class presentations in small groups, along with 1-page (single-spaced, otherwise APA) documentations of and reflections on such responses. This emerging portfolio encourages you to put aside your assumptions, and adult restraint, and playfully/powerfully indulge and participate in the world of teaching and learning (i.e., history, geography, culture, and arts)—perhaps re-experiencing the sheer beauty of language, the power of a story well-told, and the truth surprisingly revealed in an artfully-crafted picture, gesture or sound, or experiential reflection upon or critical analysis of some question, theme or issue.

It serves not only as a vehicle through which to explore your own relationship with the what, why and how of teaching social studies—and yourself as teacher and student (historian, geographer, anthropologist, social being, human being...), but also through which to participate in a number of pedagogical activities, as teachers, toward guiding children in similar explorations."

- o What is peace?
- o (Why) do we want it so badly?
- o (Why) is peace so hard to realize?
- o What does peace look like? Feel like? Sound like? Etc.
- o Is there peace or are there peaces—plurality, alterity, and difference constituting peace existentially?
- o Ought and can we educate for peace?
- o If we can educate for peace, what role can or does (social studies) curriculum and teaching play?
- o What/how might it mean to teach for peace?

I specifically, though, took these additional questions up—and engaged students in examining historical and popular images, symbols, definitions, and thoughts of peace—after students undertook this assignment, in hopes of encouraging the "beginning with me" (each's own imaginings and experiences) of peace, from which to enter into dialogue and conversation with larger, perhaps differing, peace portraits, dreams, and texts; and with each other: us, there, together, and beyond.

Yet, herein I did not assume or aspire to some objective, pure, untainted or unbiased apprehension of their peace ideas on my part, should such without question even exist; in fact, I had been engaging students in this work long before I thought to purposively study the fruit of it in this way; rather it was some of the unexpected sweet fruit borne of it, to me, that inspired further inquiry. Moreover, the students were introduced to the assignment, included in the syllabus, at the semester's start; although it was not due nor did we attend it until near the term's end, I suspect many if not most students addressed it little more than a month before. Still, additionally, many aspects of the course itself, as designed, may have led students to such questions and lines of inquiry, or at least profoundly influenced them once undertaken.

---

9 University study generally is organized via two 16-week semesters per academic year. Most classes meet for roughly two hours, once a week, in the evening for the duration of the semester. I have also offered this course in an alternate format, eight sessions of roughly four hours each, every other week.

In concert with the vision of our teacher education program, the course has shared, across sections and teachers, certain key assignments and texts: for example, a doing social-studies research project through which each student addresses an interest and gap in his or her knowledge of social studies (with an eye to larger exclusions in the existing social-studies "canon") and draws upon study findings to create a mini-curriculum unit for teaching what has been learned; and reading and discussion of Loewen's (2007) *Lies My Teacher Told Me: Everything Your American History Textbook Got Wrong*—a critical analysis of 12 mainstream school history textbooks and indictment of what teaching from them has ill-produced, and Cowhey's (2006) *Black Ants and Buddhists: Thinking Critically and Teaching Differently in the Primary Grades*—the account of an activist second-grade teacher of her efforts to critically teach for student agency toward social justice.

The inclusion of "multicultural" in the very title of the course also reflects the program's commitments to critical multiculturalism, also evidenced largely in course design. Understanding, articulating, and considering the implications of one's social/cultural location in relation to one's work as a teacher constitutes a considerable emphasis in the course as well.[10] In introducing pre-service students to

---

10 In my course, a major assignment—"Telling Tales" (Social Studies, Self and a Pedagogy of the Personal; personal life/oral history & storytelling performance)— also asks students to address their own location and history in order to reflect upon influences upon who they are as teachers, and their ideas about social studies and teaching it. This work, too, affirms certain pedagogical engagements of subjectivity in social studies education also. The assignment overview reads: "Because you teach who you are—because your personal identity is also political (culturally-constituted, complex, changing, even contradictory), implicated in the social studies curriculum and inextricably wrapped up in your professional identity—this work calls for you to study yourself, the 'you' that you bring to teaching, and to the teaching of social studies. To gain greater understanding of your own place and perspective with respect to social studies, pedagogy and curriculum, this project also asks that you conduct your own personal life/oral history research and connect its findings to a larger cultural history through the selection of a folk tale, which you will learn and tell for the class. Storytelling is a true and compelling art, indelibly tied to the history and tradition of a people. The folk tale you choose will be one that has deep meaning for you personally and connects you to your own personal life history in some way. The portfolio will comprise a number of your research findings (including 'visual aid'

curriculum development in school and community contexts in social studies including a critical examination of content and methodology, and current practices and issues in the social sciences, anti-oppressive, anti-racist education is thus particularly explored for its rich possibilities. For me, I generally take such up in my courses through the framework of critical pedagogy[11] and its call to praxis, sharing how such has influenced me, and my approach to children, teaching, and social studies.

For my classes specifically, perhaps in part due to the apprehensions I have already shared respecting the relationship between education and politics and dangers of ideological exclusivity, I ask students to explore together with me through the course the broad overarching—albeit also deeply personal—question: "How[12] does it mean (to me) to teach social studies (to children) in the elementary and middle schools?" In this way, we engage the texts above and other readings (through which I also seek to engage conflicting and/or divergent perspectives) to explore—academically, professionally, pedagogically, conceptually, autobiographically, experientially, etc.—such questions as: What does it mean to teach? Why teach? How does it mean to teach? What is social studies? Why social studies? Whose social studies? To and for whom? The "Pedagogical Play" assignments, undertaken throughout the semester, as a whole consti-

---

representations)—around 'doing' the history of you, as well as information on (and the rationale behind) the folk tale you have selected."

11 My understanding of critical pedagogy is principally grounded in the work of Freire (1970/1993) and his praxis of teaching built on humanization, justice, and the alleviation of human suffering as central to the project of education—teachers and students as subjects, not objects, in this work; "reading the word and world," attending the political relationship between knowledge and power, for greater awareness, understanding, and agency in the struggle for freedom and creation of a more just world. For further elucidation here, see Kincheloe (2004) who provides a lucid introduction to critical pedagogy.

12 The "How" is meant to engage not only the what, why, or other, but also the how respecting social studies; simply put, it asks students to consider method, manner, medium—pedagogy—in the teaching of social studies, in relation to content, substance (key commitments, questions), in articulating what social studies and teaching it to children means.

tute 20% of the final grade,[13] largely reflective of a student's full participation in the course, a primary goal therein to compel engagement with, personal appraisal of, and reflection upon the ideas set forth in course readings; and also in the way of scaffolding thought toward a final synthesis essay addressing this larger course question.

Additionally, in requiring such study before each class, I seek to maximize student voice, cultivating greater preparedness for dialogic participation. The "Picturing Peace" inquiry is but one, and the last, among some ten or more engagements herein, typically four to five of which include written responses. Among these, a student may create a portrait of a past teacher or childhood school social studies education in relation to theoretical and pedagogical orientations and questions set forth via course readings, take up a particular position to debate concerning the why or what of social studies, or brainstorm curriculum and teaching ideas for a piece of children's literature or critically analyze it in relation to issues Loewen (2007) raises concerning the subject of address (for example, Columbus and the colonization of the Americas; race, racism and anti-racism, etc.). While my syllabus has changed over the years, as has the constitution of the "Pedagogical Play" requirement, including the substance of the written pieces, I have consistently held onto the "Picturing Peace" assignment, and as a capstone concluding the "Pedagogical Play" of the semester.

The assignment—in concert with something of the theoretical and methodological foundations and frames of this, my own, interpretive inquiry in pursuit of peace—reflects my larger interest, oft undertak-

---

13 While the fact that the student work under study is part of graded course work may raise questions respecting the substance of that which students have set forth therein, such constitutes but a tenth or so of 20% of the total grade, or 2%; additionally, a student rubric is provided that broadly outlines criteria for grading written work in the course (i.e., voice, supported argument, use of literature, organization, mechanics, substance of engagement, reflection). Here, I communicate my desire for "authenticity" and openness of inquiry, a "look into and see" posture with camera respecting peace—what it looks like and means for/to you in your life as you are living it, and implications gleaned from such for the possibilities of teaching for peace (should you take this up). In this sense, there is no image or symbol or definition or implication for which I am specifically looking, or have in mind in advance, a condition of which students, too, are made aware.

en as inspired by Derrida's poststructuralist approach, which Critchley and Kearney (1997/2006) call a form of "conceptual genealogy": the work of uncovering that which is hidden and yet powerfully operative—typically multifaceted, divergent, and even contradictory—in our educational ideas, curriculum approaches, and pedagogical practices. Here, our dreams of peace. For me, this work includes inquiry into what can be gleaned via symbol, experience, memory, desire, and language. Such images and ideas, once elicited, offer rich and meaningful "data"—or in poststructuralist language, "texts" or discourses—for critical awareness and analysis potentially toward cultivating dialogue and solidarity, creative transformation, and praxis—new problems, and possibilities. For me, such is also akin to the work of *conscientization* (Freire, 1970/1993), and its study, that of the scene of subjectivity, one I seek ever to affirm, and submit, that is vital to understanding and cultivating social change and solidarity as well.

What I present here, in the following chapters, is based on my initial re-view of photographs in concert with student reflections on them, as issuing from these conceptual and pedagogical interests: a kind of effort for myself to enact a "pedagogy of seeing" (Gaudelli, 2011), and research pedagogically also in this way. Such is grounded, too, in what emerged as student pieces on peace were coded by identifying: (1) images and symbols expressed; (2) definitions and meanings articulated, including ideas and insights gleaned through such; (3) pedagogical implications presented; and (4) comments made and reflections given on the process and/or context of the inquiry itself. My intention was to first get a sense of "us together"—culling and thematically categorizing these findings to see anew just what shared, and different, dreams of peace and pedagogical possibilities for or questions concerning their realization emerged from such personalized and experiential inquiry.[14] As this "pedagogical play"

---

14 Thus, while data was organized by class cohort (semester and year, etc.), with identifications available for analysis in relation to such factors as gender and race, I did not here attend explicitly to such distinctions. I did include tallies of repetition of images, definitions and such to get a count concerning and gain a clearer picture of proportion on what was shared, and not, respecting the dream and work of peace.

was undertaken toward understanding peace in relation to one's subjectivity and lived experience, attention to such, of course, constituted an essential lens in all my readings, with an eye to noting expressions of desire, and those of ethical concern—respecting the language of peace, as well.

Herein, I chose not to focus on my own viewing of the photographs, or on the photographs as such themselves; i.e., color, line, texture, etc.; though I did seek to engage them symbolically somewhat and in relation to historical and popular images of peace. For my purposes here, I was interested mostly in how my education students, these prospective teachers, "read" their own photographs, and peace and teaching for peace in relation to them and to this "play" process—their inquiry into their own imaginings, and their re-imaginings, of peace.

Chapter 3
On Re-Imagining Peace, in Portraiture

The true mystery of the world is the visible, not the invisible.
                    -Oscar Wilde (cited in Cameron, 1992, p. 23)

The image is the most complete technique of all communication.
                    -Claus Oldenburg (cited in Cameron, 1992, p. 136)

What a beautiful fix we are in now; peace has been declared.
                    -Napoleon Bonaparte (cited in Linstroth, 2005, p. 1)

The Eye/I of Peace Dreams:
Imagination, Experience, and Subjectivity

My education students, the prospective teachers with whom I work, constitute much of the new life in my midst, the essence of education as natality within which I most directly dwell and work in my every-day professional life, and thus also to whom I ever strive to be re-sponsible/response-able. And so I begin again with them, and herein have sought not only to see them and their ideas more deeply, but also to listen more fully to that which they experience and what they glean in reflecting upon such experience. In short, I seek to learn peace from them, and learn something of the peace which they as teachers may bring to children, the new in their midst, as well; herein, first, I present education students' images and ideas of peace, and then engage prospective teachers' thoughts on peace inquiry and pedagogy. In this chapter, I focus on the photographs, and these aspiring teachers' significations of them in order to present some "representative" portraiture of how peace has been (re)-imagined by them in relation to their lived realities.

> To see the world in a grain of sand
> And heaven in a wild flower...
>   -from William Blake "Auguries of Innocence"

> The wolf shall lie down with the lamb,

and the leopard shall lie down with the kid;
and the calf and the young lion and the fatling together;
and a little child shall lead them.
        -Isaiah 11:6

Illustration 1: Sunflower and Child Celebration
Photograph by Lauren Perovich

In culling education-student/prospective-teacher images of and symbols for peace via lived experience as documented through photographs, five broad categories for organizing them emerged for me, which I present in order of strength both across and within portraits. All students presented numerous photographs falling within the first two categories—both of which were most and equally prominent: *nature* and *people*. The third grouping, attended by nearly 80% of all students, was *animals*, which could also have been included in the nature category, but were not, particularly because such were photographed and explicated in somewhat distinct ways from those referencing the natural world more explicitly or directly. Fourth, participants referenced *places of or for peace (beyond those represented in nature), and objects therein related to cultivating and supporting peace in them*. Finally, and engaged only marginally, were signifiers of peace symbols as symbols, like the peace sign or V-sign made with the hand. What is not apparent, however, in such categories, is that with respect to all of them, the reflections taken up by these prospective teachers had much to do with their relationships to and with, experiences and memories of, the aspects of nature, people, animals, places, objects, symbols, etc., presented, as well as relationships among people or animals in the photographs, for example, or in relation to another "something." To this I return, after discussing and delineating each category a bit further; and the relatively few images set forth as antitheses of peace, among other more singular articulations.

Nature

Images of *water* in nature were most abundantly shared in this category (76%), albeit in different forms. Photographs of rivers were prominent, perhaps as living or at least attending school in New York City students afforded the greatest access to water via the Hudson and East Rivers. Pictures of ocean or sea followed; lakes, waterfalls and raindrops were also present, to a much lesser extent. *Flowers* were photographed nearly as much—in this study, daffodils especially. *Trees* were included in just under half of the participants' portraits as well—with some focus herein on seeds, saplings and the act of planting trees. The *sun*—including sunset and sunrise—was depicted in one-third of student photographic collections, though when considered relative to images of *land* (field, mountain, beach) or *sky* (with rainbows), a majority of students brought to their portraits of peace some form or another of land and sky—some articulated as panoramic or scenic *views* as well: an eye to the eye, sense of taking in, beholding, a natural world of sweeping beauty, and in harmony. At least half of all students identified such photographs explicitly with the term "nature," one-third or so also contextualized as taken in *gardens* or *parks*, both natural settings involving human cultivation and presence, and also readily available for enjoyment in the city.

    A number of qualities were tied to descriptions of these images— like "beautiful" and "harmonious" as mentioned above—by a majority of prospective teachers as well: soft and quiet and simple, calm and soothing, warm and light, bright and colorful; open and new, and blossoming, emerging, growing, full and changing—and linked to spring (and Easter) as well by at least one-third of them. While one account may be found simply in the fact that students by and large undertook this inquiry in April, the latter part of a spring semester, certain meanings made and insights gleaned by them suggest there may be "more than meets the eye" here. Additionally, there remains more to be explored in expressions of contrast that were also dominantly present, the above amid that which was identified as dark, cold, hard, harried, noisy and chaotic, but also alone and solitary—for example, a brilliant green seedling sprouting up from the cold, dark ground, or a single yellow flower growing through a sidewalk crack of a busy, polluted city street.

Illustration 2: Tree amid Water and Grasses
Photograph by Lauren Perovich

People

All of these prospective teachers depicted people as a focal point in their visions of peace as well. Photographs included first and foremost those of *children*—girls, boys, students (of those student teaching at the time), daughters and sons (of those who are mothers), and a good many newborns and *babies*. Others included were identified as nieces and nephews, as well, reflecting the fact that *family* was also strongly represented, nearly as much as the young; most identified in written reflections among them were mother, father, and grandmother; with "family" explicitly used in written expression by one-third of these education students. *Friends* were also featured centrally, including roommates and classmates. While not many chose to photograph her- or himself among the "people" of peace, a few did—mostly with others, and many more "shot" objects to which they personally related in some meaningful way or to suggest activities in which they so engaged.

A number of all of these photographs also encompassed *people doing things*, and often together as well, particularly when the person featured was not identified as a child as child, or friend or family member, such that a sub-theme emerged of *people doing things they love or enjoy*, or *together* with those they love or enjoy. *Playing*, or leisurely activity, dominated such doings—for example, baseball, soccer, bocce ball, walking, riding a horse, fishing, skateboarding, entertaining (references to food, cooking, and potlucks herein), conversing over coffee. *Working*—mostly students working—was also mentioned, as related to pictures of children collaboratively doing science lab experiments, playing math games or working a puzzle, or reading. (Of course, these are prospective teachers pursuing their own portraits of peace, students working nicely perhaps a part of such aspirations!) A sizable proportion of those photos depicting people together in these ways (especially those not identified specifically as family or friends) were also notable in encompassing the theme of unity amid diversity; for example, children from all different ethnic and social backgrounds, girls and boys of differing ages playing amicably together at a park playground, and children from all different areas of the globe as depicted in the Disney World amusement ride It's a Small World.

Herein one-third of them also highlighted the import of activities (included among them, painting, drawing, dancing, and singing) that are creative, supporting *self-expression*, as well as a *sense of efficacy*, accomplishment. One prospective teacher included a photograph of herself with her monthly planner and a completed graduate essay. Another presented students smiling over their originally made tiles illustrating peace. Another photographed a royalty check she received for a book she had written on environmental issues—happy too that others had showed interest in caring for the earth, and that she could contribute to work to that end. As many also emphasized "just being together"; key words repeated most dominantly in relation to people presented included: smiling, enjoying, being, welcoming, hugging, talking, and sharing. Implicit herein—"just being," and as taken elsewhere, such as in and of nature, is paradoxically also the sense of people *not* doing, taking a break from doing, simply being, in relation to peace—meditating, another (non)activity included in such people portraits too, for example.

Certain figures were also found among the focus on people—though only by a quarter or so of education students—as symbols of, embodiments of, and/or inspirations to peace: Madonna and child, Jesus, Buddha, the Dalai Lama, the Hindu god Ganesh, and Sadako (a young girl from Japan whose story we read in class, who died due to radiation poisoning after the bombing of Hiroshima in World War II).[1] Gandhi, King, and others were also nominally identified by one student in her written reflections. Another two photographed healers in their own lives: a doctor and body worker/massage therapist. One photographed a newspaper clipping about the female Columbia student who was tortured for hours in her apartment by her rapist, yet survived the ordeal and lived to tell her story, heal, and help others. Respecting such figures, qualities of compassion, courage, determination, perseverance, faith, or sacrificial love were highlighted—*beacons of hope* amid such things as desperation, suffering, war, violence, oppression, and injustice.

---

1 See Eleanor Coerr, *Sadako and the Thousand Paper Cranes* (New York: BDD Books, 1979).

Illustration 3: Peace Friends and Laughing Toddler
Photograph by Eunice Yun

Animals

In featuring animals in photographic entries into peace, half of the 80% of prospective teachers who did so presented two or more animals in each portrait, or an animal with a person, emphasizing in writing the aspect of being together and in relation. Among these animals most prominent were *birds*, including a few cranes (also symbolically important in relation to the Sadako book we read in class), and doves, as well as a bird's nest, and eggs. Nearly as represented were animals identified as *pets*—mostly cats and dogs; yet also a few goldfish and turtles in the sun, albeit these not pets with any certainty. An injured pigeon finding refuge in a park corner was also among those featuring animals. A favorite activity shown and commented upon for pets was sleeping, many seen nestled together on bed or floor or couch. Some students linked children and animals together through the ideas of innocence, pure joy, and unconditional love, as well.

Illustration 4: Happy Puppy
Photograph by Lauren Perovich

Peace Places (Beyond Nature) and Objects Supporting
Peace Presence Therein

Home—"a room of one's own"—was the place most identified—beyond those spaces denoting the natural world and dwelling therein and amid or in view of nature—by education students as one of peace for them; in fact, half of them included home amid their photographs to picture peace. For some, this was the city apartment in which they presently lived, although at least a quarter of them also turned to homes of origin outside New York City as well, and in concert with the idea that peace would be hard to find in the city—an initial belief challenged in most of them through the course of their inquiries. Albeit a minority, the prospective teachers who brought forth images designed to communicate the antithesis of peace included photos of the homeless, or refugees or immigrants longing for home. Objects related to home were also found among these presentations: bed and/or couch, affiliated most with sleep and rest; window, linked to light and a view to the world outside; fire in a fireplace, for warmth and light and quiet reflection; vase with flower(s) and/or work(s) of art, to behold the presence of beauty; and a stack of books and other graduate-student materials, for the joy of studying, of attending meaningful inquiry and aspiration. A few clocks were among these objects present too, with an eye to time itself as space and place, as well, for peace. Allied with a sense of comfort, control, and amenable structure, also included were a few calendars, monthly planners, and an ordered arrangement of colored pencils for drawing.

A good third of students depicted what we might glean to be art beyond the art object as such, or perhaps a panoramic view of beauty of a sort analogous to that nature affords, with photographs of the cityscape—including fountains, buildings of pronounced architectural design and other aesthetic portraits of *the city* via its streets, landmarks, and sidewalks, and shoes required for being in, traversing, the city—from which to take in its sights. Several shoes showed up (and with iPod), particularly in relation to walking and running, as meditative, stress-reducing supports for peace, and affording freedom of movement and perspective, or new or enlarged view. Language describing these photos also pointed to the import of places to behold, reflect, enjoy, and in which "to lose oneself." And the city, at least for most of them at the time of the inquiry, was also a kind of home for them perhaps too, the place they presently inhabited and in which they lived.

Churches, synagogues, and other *places for religion or spirituality* were pictorially referenced by nearly one-fifth of all prospective teachers. Such were identified as places to pray, meditate, worship, give thanks, celebrate, build relationships, enjoy community, and intend and contend for peace. Related objects included not only religious figures already previously noted but also lotus, mandala, prayer beads, kneeler, cross, stained-glass window, and church door. One prospective teacher who practices meditation included a head-less statue of the Buddha accompanied with the idea that she, anyone, could be Buddha. Most depicted herein though, interestingly, were images related to music—flutes and other instruments, and choirs singing and concerts underway—highlighting harmonious and uplifting sound and song. One Jewish student raised issues respecting religion, politics, history, and peace via a photograph on the cover of an *Economist* magazine depicting Israel as the key to peace.

A few *additional places*, although by less than 10%, were featured amid this collection of photographs as well: cars, signifying freedom and control (as explained by those who included them); classrooms (or school science lab), signifying community, inquiry, and learning; and cemeteries, signifying rest, quiet and the peace of death. Howev-er, when memorials to peace or for honoring those who fought for peace are included herein, about one-fifth of education students addressed places commemorating those who have passed.

Illustration 5: City Skyline
Photograph by Lauren Perovich

Symbols of Peace as Symbols

Only a very few, by a very few, symbols of peace were among the photographs submitted; from the *peace sign* or logo and V-sign hand gesture, to *religious icons* and figures (like Buddha), and animals (like the *dove*), as symbols. The *American flag*, too, was also among such symbols. One flag was found nestled between a Tasos Café and a Greek restaurant, the presence of diverse peoples living together affirmed. One prospective teacher photographed a police vehicle with respect to a world where law is required and agreed upon to keep the peace. Actual signs were also depicted by some as reflective of some aspect of peace upon which they reflected in writing: a Quiet Zone sign, a sign reminding drivers to share the road with cyclists, a Metro-North posted danger warning, and a pro-peace display. Perhaps given the nature of the assignment, the peace sought and expressed through photographs directed education students to images of peace gleaned from the particular contexts of their lived experiences, of concrete specificity, rather than to picturing peace in the abstract or as envisioned via popular icons and media.

Picturing Peace's Opposite and Other Eyes/I's on Possibilities for Portraying Peace

While the majority of education students did not choose to present images deemed antithetical to peace in their portfolios, among those present, in addition to depictions of homelessness or displacement, others in this vein included images of pollution and litter; one, of New York City crowds as stressful and noisy; and another, of Times Square as a terrorist target inciting fears over safety. Some also photographed images of wars, riots, or other acts of violence (in print or historical documentation). Three students undertaking this inquiry in the spring of 2007, if not introducing images thereof, grounded their inquiries into peace in relation to the tragic shooting at Virginia Polytechnic Institute and State University ("Virginia Tech"). Celia[2]

---

2 All education student names introduced in this essay are pseudonyms.

(4/20/07), a career-changer and mother in her forties, begins her reflection in this manner:

> This isn't a good week for peace. Spring is making a tempestuous appear-
> ance, leaving 8 inches of rain in the basement. Radicals in Iraq are winning
> as more bodies pile up. The Virginia Tech massacre is nearly impossible to
> reconcile with peace. It's unbearable to think of those mothers and fathers of
> dead students. But more chilling, in the long run, is that a human being
> chooses to *pacify* his demons by executing this horror. This is the antithesis
> of peace.

Tara (4/20/07) reflects upon her own initial portraits of peace expressive of her need and enjoyment of, as well as desire for, sleep and relaxation in light of the university violence, highlighting what she calls her own selfishness, and includes a photo of Cho Seung-Hui, the student perpetrator of the shooting, as the embodiment of peace's antithesis. Herein she also articulates qualities involving profound and unaddressed suffering, alienation and isolation, and fullness of hatred (including self-hatred) as at odds with peace. Adrianne (4/19/07), a Korean American student, also includes in her profile a photo of this student and comments thus:

> It would be unfair of me to write this peace assignment without mention-
> ing.... The Virginia Tech University incident made me realize how fragile
> peace is.... I feel safe when I am on campus...shocking...such an event oc-
> curred in a setting that is usually...a safe haven. In addition, there is great
> fear by the Korean community of a racially driven backlash simply because
> the perpetrator was a South Korean national. I read in the New York Times
> today how as a result of this event, some Korean American students are
> being bullied by their classmates at school....

Chloe (4/22/08) included among her photos one of a young boy, a student, making the peace V-sign with one hand, while holding a toy gun in the other. She pointed to our confusion as an obstacle to peace, and our "desire to be at peace, while finding the need to arm ourselves against others." Katherine (4/24/06) seemed, in a substantial number of her images, to focus on certain obstacles to peace as well, and as reminders of such, and of those things crucial to the maintenance, cultivation, and/or restoration of peace. A liquor store signified the ways in which we may seek peace by drugs through escape or unconsciousness; and she also counted the number of liquor stores near the school in which she was student teaching, a low-income neighborhood different from her own with far more such stores in just a three-block radius. Her portrait of her grandmother's pills, in contrast, signified the ways in which drugs can sustain and support life, a sign of care for quality of life in old age.

In her photograph of her grandmother in her wheelchair, however, Katherine also spoke of her grandmother's troubling relation to her memories as expressed in the repetition of certain stories, and the human need to "make peace with the past" for present peace. Relatedly, she included a picture of the door to the room she had growing up; the door had a nail that once hosted a "Keep Out" sign. For her, the image conjured memories of the many door-slamming fights she had with her sister throughout her youth. This reminded her of the import of communication (she also included an image of a telephone amid her photos), conflict resolution, negotiating difference and disagreement, forgiveness, and social responsibility, even and especially in one's close relationships. While I am seeking here to present less collectively represented or more singularly presented images as related to picturing peace, or those grounded in some unique framing, I did find that a majority of prospective teachers referenced memories (albeit mostly good ones), "looking back," looking again and anew, respecting the photos presented, whether of a ten-year reunion with former classmates and old friends, beach scene taken while on vacation, festive occasion with family, or moment of joy and appreciation experienced alone on a busy city street.

Chloe (4/22/08) not only confirmed a communicative aspect to peace, but also a sense of contrast in her image of a telephone pole seen hazily in the midst of a dark fog. Ruth's (4/24/06) profile of peace particularly emphasized the presence of contrasting elements—peace, to her, defined ever in relation to its absence or opposite. Many of her photos were grouped in juxtaposing pairs: an artfully presented graffiti wall, and a fence freshly painted to "remove" the work of vandals; young parents at church bringing their children to be baptized, and two young girls lovely in their Easter best but "acting up" and causing a disturbance in the service; and a baby sleeping beside an image of an "exhausted" dad on the floor trying to sleep while his young daughter crawled on him, "demanding attention." Ruth also included singular images encompassing key contrasts, as well, like a photograph of a musician in the subway amid "hustling and bustling" activity of passersby, "quietly playing Pacobel's Canon D," unnoticed by many.

Seeking peace anew, in this way, through attending to and capturing images of peace and the experience of peace within their own lives, these prospective teachers also began a journey of noticing the before unnoticed, at least for and by many of them. With these images, and the symbols and portraits and ideas and dreams of peace generated from and through them, they were then able to describe peace anew, first for themselves, and then for others, and in relation to their work as teachers. Undertaking thus a kind of descriptive inquiry into peace, each articulated for herself, or himself, through such disciplined observation of the phenomenon from the site of his or her own subjectivity the meanings of peace lived and made therein. It is to this meaning-making, this re-conceptualizing of peace, as presented in their reflective writings, to which I now turn in Chapter 4.

Chapter 4
A Word Worth a Thousand Pictures

We will not have peace by afterthought.
                    -Norman Cousins (1956)

Every day we do things, we are things that have to do with peace. If we are aware of our life..., our way of looking at things, we will know how to make peace right in the moment, we are alive.
                    -Thich Nhat Hanh (1992, p. 112)

Peace, Subjectively Lived, Experienced, Defined

I have begun with these prospective teachers' photographs as a window into gleaning something of their dreams of peace, as imagined and lived, particularly because symbols and images often communicate in powerful, rich, and untold ways the meanings and experiences we bring to our understandings of and practices regarding that to which they refer, in this case: peace. Additionally, these visual presentations afforded my education students the opportunity to reflect on such in their own lives, and potentially in relation to their work as teachers of children, and articulate these thoughts in written form. For me here, both via images captured and symbols invoked as well as written discussions of them, a plethora of possibilities are potentially made available, by study, for re-imagining and pursuing peace anew.

Among the most well-known traditional images as symbols for peace[1] are the dove, affiliated with the soul in India, love in the Greek and sacred to Aphrodite, and forgiveness and reconciliation with God in Judeo-Christian lore; the olive branch[2] (or tree or oil), signifying

---

1 See: Biedermann, 1994; Fontana, 1993; Hope, 1997.

2 The olive traditionally among some cultures has been a strong source of sustenance, healing, and delightful taste. Additionally, the Old Testament story of the flood features well-known images of peace, the olive branch among them, with dove and rainbow—and a promise by Yahweh to never again in anger at human evil flood the earth.

victory and healing from Greek times, and allied with Athena the goddess of wisdom and war; the laurel wreath, also of victory, and for cleansing the soul, and sacred to Apollo the god of reason; and Sapphire, a precious jewel, denoting veracity and charity, and known to be blue as the heavens, thus bringing purity, joy, harmony, and blessed communion—for alchemists, also healing as a poison remedy. In ancient China, clouds (generally five) were also commonly so symbolic, communicating a union of opposites—herein particularly, between East and West (Biedermann, 1994; Hope, 1997; Fontana, 1993). While the photographs submitted by these prospective teachers certainly did not reproduce these images in large measure, much that they did produce were related, resonated with other related ancient symbols, and/or evoked meanings akin to both.

Though only a few doves were represented (and pigeons, related to the dove), birds were abundantly found—from ancient times, of major symbolic and sacred significance (Biedermann, 1994; Hope, 1997) referencing: spirit, freedom, flight, heaven, gods and goddesses, communication (used as messengers), fidelity and fertility (related to love and marriage in tenderness and nesting instinct), healing (used sacrificially for such) and longevity, the ascent of the soul and immortality (especially the crane, which was engaged by a number of education students). Kurt, also a musician, who created a photo-essay for this project, framed his inquiry in this way: "All of these photos were taken in one day—Thursday, April 19, 2007, I woke up and heard the bird singing" (4/20/07). None of these additional well-known traditional symbols for peace as peace—that is, olive branch, laurel wreath, blue sapphire, or cloud—were depicted or referenced by participants in this "picturing peace" project, yet related, and perhaps more readily existentially present, images from nature—trees and plants, the blues of water and sky, and clouds as related to sky and water as well, were found among them.

Water, which was most present, albeit in manifold forms, in these "pictures" of peace, for instance, has traditionally been accredited with magical properties, known as a source of transformation and healing, and as a symbol for the soul—manifest in whatever form and however many different forms: purifying, renewing, sustaining life. The gods and goddesses were also believed to find their dwelling places near or in water—thus, the baptism or christening with water of some religious faiths; and the lotus flower, as a lily, grows in water, signifying in Buddhist thought the "flowering" of the soul or enlightenment. Other images confirmed such ideas/ideals as well: for example, those related to spring, home, children, family, and play, work, and rest of various sorts.

Sky, of course, with whom the bird finds kinship, albeit intangible, carries the breath of god and hope of freedom. With images of sun as life-giving and beneficent, and light and fire as source of light and warmth and traditionally reflecting divinity's essence, prospective teachers here also summoned symbols of the soul—unseen and insubstantial and yet necessary for life, spirit, prana, the vitality of the life force; and freedom and inspiration as well as illumination. Further photographs presented also confirmed such ideas, whether via a car, calendar (also from ancient times, sacred, honoring life's cycles and seasons) or planner, running shoe, game or graduate essay. Additionally, rainbows stretching across the sky, as featured in some "Picturing Peace" images and also amid clouds, not only find reference to the promise of Yahweh to never again flood the earth in anger at humanity's evil ways, but also to the Buddhist and Hindu tantric idea of the rainbow body signifying the attainment of the highest meditative state of which the human in this life is capable (Hope, 1997).

Participant references in manifold ways to the earth or land, also revered from ancient times as home to deities—especially mountains and trees, affirmed a symbolic embrace of the creative powers of the universe, life's cycles and seasons, a sense of enduring affiliation amid change. Trees, as well, rooted and reaching, are linked with regeneration and grounding, not only being powerfully present but also present to becoming and to having been—reflecting our spiritual identity, and also the spirits of our ancestors, visiting or dwelling there. The lone tree speaks also of shamanic tests of spiritual capacity requiring endurance. Landscapes, too, encompassed in the vistas and views portrayed, signify power and protection, hearkening back to the earth as the mother, and home, of all. Interestingly, some of the animals featured in the work of prospective teachers corroborate such meanings of peace further: for example, turtles signifying earth or cosmos, cats symbolizing motherhood, fertility and sex or intimacy in Ancient Egypt, and even dogs as "man's best friend."

Similarly, images of spring or child, among others, enjoy strong and deeply symbolic histories in human civilizations across the globe from ancient times. These illuminate but a few examples of the rich meanings excavated, many perhaps unwittingly, in the photographs these prospective teachers took in response to the call to pursue "peace." Additionally, many of their photographs find affiliation or resonate with popular, contemporary images of peace; as gleaned simply from a few online Google searches, these include the well-known international peace sign and logo and peace V-sign hand gesture,[3] the healing hand, a child smiling or children, people in protest against war and related signs and banners of power and resistance, a rainbow-like flag—both the Italian "PACE" peace flag, and that used by gay communities, the earth's globe (oft cradled by human hands), a still water view (such as of a lake), a starry night or sunny blue sky (sometimes with rainbow), a peace lily, a dove (sometimes in human hands), cranes, and a lit candle.

While neither time nor space affords addressing such in further breadth or depth or greater number here, before turning explicitly to the further meanings actually made by prospective teachers themselves as gleaned in their written discussions of and reflections upon

---

3The use of the V-sign hand gesture signifying "V" for victory emerged in the context of war, popularized especially in World War II. Critically taken up by anti-war advocates, like John Lennon, in the 1960s, particularly in protest against the Vietnam War, it was embraced as a symbol for peace. The triangular three-lined encircled peace sign of today finds its origins most directly in a symbol constructed by Nicolas Roerich, in concert with a movement to protect cultural and historical artifacts and institutions, adopted in 1935 in a pact made by the U.S. and Latin American nations committing to such protection in times of peace and war. This banner of peace (three solid circles in a larger circle) was said to draw from symbols of ancient origins acknowledging the triune and sacred nature of human existence (i.e., past, present, and future; art, science and religion). The first use of the sign as we know it today dates back to 1958, in the design of a ceramic peace badge for the Campaign for Nuclear Disarmament (a combination of original V in victory and N & D), a British disarmament movement, which the anti-war movement subsequently took up, as well as other movements for peace. For more on this history, see Kolsbun & Sweeney, 2008.

the visual presentations they generated, another thread of historical symbolic meaning picked up by prospective teachers deserves mentioning: those engaging peace specifically in relation to its absence or opposite, or via juxtaposing contrasts or the reconciliation of such. David Fontana (1993) in his explication of traditional symbols for peace speaks of them only in relation to war, oppositional to peace as hell's visitation, beauty's violation, and disturbance and destruction; psychically, in this way, peace is contrasted with mental turmoil, madness, and the human battle between desires base and exalted. Thus, Fontana, also aligning separation, fragmentation, and aggression with the masculine, and rites of initiation into manhood, affiliates peace with that which is feminine—that which is fertile and healing; creates, renews, restores, brings together and nurtures life; harbinger also of maturity of mind and receptivity, and reconciliation and integration of differing and oppositional forces or elements. This idea of harmony certainly came through, in manifold ways, in education-student photographs and choices made in discussing them—unacknowledged homage perhaps to the (Roman) goddess of peace, called Pax or Harmony, and sometimes featured with a lion as well, as lion-hearted, courage required of her too.

Interestingly, the *Oxford English Dictionary* (*OED*, 1989) also dominantly grounds its defining of peace in negative terms, in relation to its opposite—*freedom from* such things as: civil disorder or unrest; dissention or contention between or among persons (which could also include a quarrel between God and an individual, particularly in its early known uses); turmoil, anxiety, or inner conflict (inclusive of spiritual, emotional, and mental states); external interference or disturbance (often respecting the condition of an individual); and hostility or war. Peace is also denoted in relation to the *absence or cessation of* such things, additionally, as movement, activity, or noise. Only following and in alignment with these particular definitions is peace signified in positive, affirmative terms, respecting what peace is rather than what it is not: public security and order; concord, amity, and a friendly state; tranquility and calm; quiet and stillness; and peacetime (state of community or nation not at war with another). The only meaning articulated for peace, though, wholly apart from and not directly attached to some presentation of its opposite or absence is one referencing a person who fosters and/or embodies harmony, concord, peace—the term peace used in the very definition here as well. Additionally referenced herein is: an agreement, treaty, ratification, of peace between communities, nations, peoples, once at war; and a salutation or expression of well-wishing, as in "peace be with you."

In highlighting etymological aspects of the multilinguistic history of the word "peace," the *OED* elucidates further something of its richness of and potential meaning(s): Beginning in ca. 1140, it identifies peace as drawn from *pak*, meaning "fasten," and related to *pacisci* signifying "to covenant or agree," replacing Old English *frið*, also *sibb*, which also meant "happiness." Dating back to ca. 1200, peace is also found to be used in various greetings; and from c. 1300, from the biblical Latin *pax*, and Greek *eirene*, which were used by translators to render Hebrew *shalom*, peace properly here related to "safety, welfare, prosperity." *Mir*, from Russian, literally meant "peace, world," and also "village, community"; from Proto-Slavic *miru*—"commune, joy, peace" (also possibly taken from Iranian origins); and the base *mei-* "to bind." *Miru* is also reported to have been "used in Christian terminology as a collective 'community of peace,'" related to translating Greek *kosmos*, "the known world, mankind."

While education-student portraits of peace are not at all at odds with this rich and multilayered history, expressive of manifold meanings and definitions that embrace many if not most of these historical legacies and formal denotations, their manner of approach made also for a different rendering of peace, particularly as embodied in human life.

Peace as Temporally, Sensuous-ly,[4] Engaged Experience— Experienced Consciously

Via this experiment in pursuing peace, prospective teachers were compelled to not only "picture" peace—foregrounding image, view

---

4 My use of this term with the hyphen is meant to offset the "sensual" as commonly conceived: here, students' highlighted heightened sensory engagement and awareness in reflecting on their lived meanings of and for peace.

and sight—but also consider it in relation to experience and to inquiry, subjectively engaged. In this way, dominant emphases that
emerged respecting the meaning of peace in relation to such may
have had more or as much to do with the pedagogical assignment
framing this work/"play" than a particular conceptualization of or
signification for peace. Still, important to set such forth here for as
faithful as possible a rendering of participant ideas, I begin thus with
this groundwork upon which the overwhelming majority of education students sought to articulate what peace meant to them: namely,
that peace itself is *an experience*, in which the *senses are engaged* in some
heightened or visceral or distinct/ distinguishable way—the *sense of
sight* most referenced; and an experience one—each, every, many,
all—*must actually choose to pursue*, actively, intentionally, consciously,
in order to realize.

Among key words highlighted in relation to this defining foundation of peace, beyond these already articulated, included: see, watch,
behold, look, notice, observe, seek, listen, find, dedicate, commit, act,
effort, and awareness. Peace conceived in this way, as an experience,
was ever apprehended respecting one's relation to, and/or relationships in, such experience, as well. In seeking, thus, to gather, glean,
elucidate, and expound upon the understandings herein constitutive,
and as articulated by participants via their written reflections, this
organization of meanings emerged for me for their presentation
here—peace as this experience: (1) of being, "in time"; (2) qualified as
desirable and affirmative in nature; (3) characterized by what I call a
sense of "with-ness"; and (4) calling for an ethics of responsibility[5] in
the midst of contexts oft antithetical to knowing and living and
learning peace.

Of Being, "In Time"

Seeing peace as an attainable state of being that has been reached for thou-
sands of years reminds me that my act of meditation connects me to the energy and consciousness of many people who have meditated before me.... I

---

5 Initially, I was drawn to depicting this word as response-ability to emphasize
capacity for response herein.

think that if each person in this world tried to demonstrate their [sic] own
belief of peace... we would be much closer to living in a less violent world.
(Elizabeth, 3/02/08)

Nearly three-quarters of education students in seeking to define peace
in some way wrote explicitly of peace as a state of being, about
simply "being," or as something embodied and experienced—noting
the import of the senses—in a way of living as a way of being. Half of
all education students further described peace as a feeling and/or
emotion; as well as space, place, and/or moment of: energy, vastness,
openness, presence, rootedness or grounding, newness, potential or
possibility, remembrance and direction. The temporality by which
peace seems to be perceived engages past, present, and future in
seeking to balance change and consistency, memory and imagination,
endurance and renewal, mind and body—and even soul and spirit;
perhaps, too, to bring together and integrate differing forces con-
fronted in the process of living.

There is a strong thrust respecting a future orientation, one that
involves hope and evolution—peace intimately tied up with the
experience and expectation of change, growth, emergence, transformation. And while one-third of prospective teachers also discuss
peace centrally in relation to history and remembrance—calling to
mind good times with family or friends or in nature from the past, or
a past in need of healing, for example; another one-third emphasize
the fact that peace simply is, is ever available, there for the experiencing now in the present moment, should we but choose to enter into it.
Herein, too, while heart and body are addressed by one-fourth of
these participants—soul by but a few, spirit by nearly half; "mind"
finds a fundamental place for nearly all of them in their ideas about
peace as related to the temporal experience of being, words found in
most texts: mind, remind, think, rethink, thought, awareness, "stop,
pause and reflect."

Expressed, herein, in relation to peace as an experience, are the
multiple aspects of bracketing experience—or even slowing it down,
consciously or meta-cognitively reflecting on experience, and, even
somewhat paradoxically, experiencing experience so fully as to lose
self-consciousness, at least, in such moments. These ideas "reminded"
me of a conversation between characters in Thornton Wilder's 1937

Pulitzer Prize–winning play *Our Town* (2007), wherein one asks another if she thinks anyone really lives or knows life—every minute—while he or she actually lives it, and the other responds that perhaps saints and poets sometimes do.

Such figures—perhaps as students of the natural world, or nature human or divine, and the relationships and their own relationships pertaining thereto—may be described as connoisseurs of experience, or as gifted in crystallizing experience in some way to its fullest or deepest expression. Another affiliated aspect of this idea of peace as such a state of being, and experience, articulated in some way by nearly all prospective teachers was what I might call a sense of efficacy—expressed via ideas like "focus and flow," creativity, confidence, direction, control, power, achievement, accomplishment, and capability. In this, the work of Mihaly Csikszentmihalyi (1990), a leading researcher in the field of "positive psychology," was also called to mind, whose empirical studies of human experience in its positive dimensions led him to what he called a "process of total involvement with life...*flow*" (p. xi), accompanied by a felt state of ecstasy and optimality, unification and creation of meaning, and in which time also actually sometimes seemed to disappear.

Possibly, some of what has been outlined thus far could describe almost any experience, or at least many kinds of experiences—maybe particularly positive ones. Perhaps peace is then a characteristic or outcome of, experienced or felt in, such experiences. How can we—really, why should we, or should we want, to focus on or choose "peace" among them? While the language of ethics certainly comes into play here in prospective-teacher discussions, as prominent, if not more so, is the language of desire: peace is not only an experienced state of being—whether felt in time or as timeless, beyond time somehow—that finds kinship with many other human virtues and ideals, but also it feels decidedly good; it is an optimal state of being, and as experienced.

Of the Optimal and Affirmative

What I loved about this assignment was the fact that it made me curious again, looking at the world through a child's eyes, finding meaning and pleasure in the little, insignificant things that often go unnoticed. (Hannah, 4/24/06)

While peace as something of *the absence of* that which is undesirable, less than optimal, negative and negating, and even painful or evil was present in education-student reflections on the meanings of peace gleaned from their lived experience as documented via photography, the heart of each and every one of their reflections actually pulsated strongly with expressions of affirmation and positive "positivity." Even in those aspects drawn upon to define peace in relation to that which opposes it, peace was described as that which delivers one from such opposition; that is, "freedom from" violence, worry, illness, fear, stress, destruction, oppression, confusion, war, conflict, thought-lessness, meaninglessness, and ignorance—woes that I identify here in the order in which they were principally found spoken of in these reflections, violence or nonviolence addressed in about 25% of them and the others in varying degrees slightly less. The pre-eminent and chief "goods" in relation to which peace was defined were joy, enjoyment, pleasure, and happiness (contentment too, but much less so), all participants taking up one or more of such descriptors—though desire, want, passion, or longing were only explicitly refer-enced by a little more than 25% of them.

Along with such delight, all brought to peace's portrait the be-stowing upon its recipient of *feelings of calm*, serenity, and/or tran-quility; and/or the creation of *places of quiet*, relaxation, ease, rest and/or stillness, even solitude. Relatedly, such places were identified with and as those of refuge, escape, haven, and sanctuary; offering also comfort, safety, strength, courage, stability, and grounding—articulated by a few as where they could again "get centered" or find their centers. Several included notions of health and healing; and abundance, richness, and prosperity; as well as appeals to feelings of wonder or perceptions of the wondrous.

Nearly as dominant among the meanings generated respecting peace were affiliations with: *hope*, linked with confidence by a few and the fresh and new by many more; *love*, compassion and care, for some sacrificial; *beauty* and the beautiful; and *harmony* and the har-monious—by 60 to 75% of participants. To a lesser extent—among one-third or so of education students—innocence (including that described as pure, unblemished, untouched, untainted), simplicity and respect (attention to worth and value too) were referenced in conceptualizations of peace. Additionally, the "power" of peace or peace as powerful was explicitly addressed by almost half of all participants—peace akin to power, control, purpose, meaning, and satisfaction amid stress.

Related to a state of being deemed experientially "good" or to experiences that feel good—as much as peace revealed itself to be affirmative, desirable, and optimal; peace was also identified with felt good, goodness, or the good, along with a number of other human virtues or ideals—perhaps even powers—by a quarter of prospective teachers, virtues such as: knowledge and understanding; justice, fairness and equity; truth (including the authentic, real, honest and non-artificial); freedom and faith. Within most understandings of peace articulated, of course, context played a key role as well, acknowledged explicitly by many education students, in the unique experiences of and singularity of meanings for peace set forth as optimal and affirmative. Context was inevitably constituted by crucial and defining relationships with others as well.

Of a Sense of "With-ness"

> I have found through working on this picturing peace project how connected I am to the environment and world around me. (Kara, 4/20/07)

"Connection" was a central word recurring throughout most prospective teachers' portraits of peace. Relationships, particularly the experiences and gifts of friendship, companionship, and camaraderie, were spoken of explicitly by more than 90% of education students. The word "with" itself—bringing together persons and cultures, establishing human relationships in and to the world, life before and beyond, animal and plant life, spirit, spirituality and God, activity and the self—noticeably peppered each written reflection on peace in numerous places of address. Words in use, in concert with this pronounced sense of with-ness elucidated through the experience of peace, included share, together, gather, support, community, closeness, journey, cooperation, solidarity, inner, and within. Nearly all participants spoke in some way of unity or unifying experience, as well, in relation to peace, albeit particularly involving unity amid difference, diversity and variety. This kind of with-ness, or one-ness—diversity-in-unity as some described it, encounter and engagement with difference, was also clearly affirmative, uplifting, sustaining, treasured, pleasurable, and desirable; and it also called for an ethics of responsibility, each taking his or her part in attending to cultivating such with-ness in conditions that all too often separate, divide, and alienate.

Calling for an Ethics of Responsibility in a World in Want of Peace

In a world where so many new developments seem to make our lives busier, more complicated, or more dangerous, we need to remember that the power to change these things lies within us. Whether we work to save the South American rainforest or the tiny church courtyard down the street, action toward peace makes the garden of our world more productive and beautiful. (Debbie 4/20/07)

Responsibility, highlighting the human capacity and demand upon us to respond in a world greatly in want of peace, was a dominant theme among prospective teachers in their written reflections on peace. In this, the language of ethics is strong, in reference to our relationship to each other and with the life world. Moreover, well over half of these education students referencing self here, a powerful site for the production and presence of peace was found first from within one's own subjectivity and personal posture toward self, other, and world. Herein peace was linked to choice, intention, dedication, effort, action, activity, reflection, generosity, appreciation, and celebration. Peace was something to offer, give, and maintain. It could be found if sought, involving also pausing, listening, acceptance, dreaming, and voice. Regarding the self, it required staying true to, knowing, opening up, and finding peace first in oneself—and connecting oneself to others, to that which is beyond the self but of which the self is really ever a part.

Peace was interestingly described here by some respecting a sense of "own-ness"—the import of time or balance or care for oneself asserted—and also of the "we-ness" or with-ness of sharing oneself, acknowledging one's impact and effect on others, and in acts of selflessness. Peace could, though, be easily lost, in relation to losing oneself, too, amid the complications of living and hectic pace of life. A world context at odds with, even hostile to, the experience of peace was painted in this way in the majority of these portraits as well—difficulty, tragedy, suffering, adversity, struggle, illness, war, destruction, worry, violence, evil, confusion, and indifference referenced in addition to stress, over-stimulation and intensity of input. As such, awareness, important for the realization of peace, was essential to countering cultures and habits of unconsciousness as lived. Herein, peace requires too, according to some 98% of these participants, a personal and collective response embodying some kind of resistance, critique, and creative praxis: overcoming, rebuilding, renewal, rebirth, and transcendence—among the words they take up.

The I/Eye in Inquiry—Subjective Source of Peace and of Pedagogy

Through this inquiry, many education students reported realizing how multifaceted peace actually is—unexpectedly found on so many levels and in abundant moments of living; and addressed through such a range: abstract, embodied, etc. Some articulated the expectation that peace would be hard to find, especially in New York City, or that such might be discovered via some dramatic display happened upon in the course of inquiry. Others began with the idea that they knew what peace was and would simply set out to capture it photographically. A shared finding for them, however, based on their peace pursuit actually involved a rethinking of, and new views on, peace for themselves—some reporting it as experientially found where least expected, others as constantly occurring should one just stop and notice it; because so simple, this intricate harmony we tend to take for granted. Those who initially found living in New York City antithetical to a life of peace found their views of the city actually changing as well, and their ideas of peace in relation to this—with a new focus on the "peace potential" of the city itself, transformed from being perceived of and experienced as crowded and noisy to vitalizing and pregnant with possibility; herein peace was about accepting new and different surroundings, learning to find and make time for visiting quiet havens therein, reading on the subway, appreciating the pace and people and visions of architectural beauty encountered, and opening one's eyes and really observing amid the hustle and bustle of city life.

In this way, the constitutive and defining importance of context, and time, was also explicitly recognized by many and implicitly noted by others. Some of those student teaching, for example, emphasized that with so much work and so little sleep in their present lives, the need and desire, even craving, for sleep and rest became preeminent, had taken on heightened meaning in relation to their images and ideas of peace. Likewise, days filled with noise, which had one longing for quiet, made perhaps even looking at the photographs of peace taken a source of quiet and peace. Several education students highlighted the value of the very opportunity to think about something they had never explicitly perhaps thought about before, especially peace beyond definition but as related to their life experience, and to examine their own existence in relation to peace. Some realized the role of faith, and following what they believed to be right to the best of their ability—a response to an irony of finding peace in knowing what to expect, in constancy, and realizing that teaching is all about change, wherein very often one never knows what to expect. Others also found the busy, even hectic, reflected in some images among their own photographs; commenting that amid such a felt sense of safety was still present, a balance of chaos and order, or joy and delight.

Relatedly, a few prospective teachers contrasted their ideas of peace with those that are codified, seeming somewhat superficial and meaningless, or merely serve as a façade for peace, as in America, a backyard, white picket fence or apple pie might. The claim was made by many, in fact, that one must experience peace in order to truly know its meaning, that it was realized daily in small measure, at least, in the course of living, amid our daily struggles; that peace is grounded in the everyday, each breath, every moment, the present now in which one lives—which also actually serves to highlight, for them, the significance of daily life, and I might add, subjectivity, one's subjective experience of it.

I have been taking photographs for as long as I can remember. Rarely have I ever thought about the topic of peace in my works.... I have attempted to capture the essence of our fragile existence—the emotional vulnerability, the physical frailty, the spiritual uncertainty. Thus I initially found this assignment to be a challenge, but as I started shooting, it became more and more natural to look for the peaceful.... I have always loved photography...a special art for it allows us to see who we are, to capture what it is to be human and share our lives with other beings and creatures on this earth... memorialize instances which give us pleasure...   (Chloe, 4/20/08)

One loves photography; another hates it, and reports initial difficulty with the assignment, feeling conspicuous, like a tourist, in her own life with a camera. Kara (4/20/07) is drawn to nature, which is then where she begins in her search for peace. Another education student envies nature's creatures that seem to enjoy the peace the river affords fully whereas she feels limited to the surface of its vastness. Another turns to the Christian Bible, and religious images, for understanding peace —religion, she says, a big part of her life since childhood. A Buddhist student grounds her portrait of peace in a conference of Muslims, who in seeking to explain their religion to others invited the Dalai Lama to join them, as she explains—Muslim in the post-9/11 world seems to symbolize violence whereas the Dalai Lama is a symbol of peace. Another, a self-identified political activist, organizes her thought around notions of home as well as law and justice—issues of homelessness in one of the world's richest countries, and the acceptance of some government control and even violence for the prospect of peace.

Herein are but a few of the insights and reflections students brought about the peace and pedagogical work of "picturing peace" in their own growth and learning and understanding—with, despite and perhaps because of all their singularities and differences of identity, experience, perspective, etc., nearly unanimous attention to the primacy of the subjective, of experience, and the context in and through which peace is sought, understood, and practiced. From these meanings, these prospective teachers then sought to consider and re-consider the possibilities for teaching peace to children in their classrooms.

Chapter 5
On the Way of / to Peace

But peace...lies in the hearts and minds of all people. So let us...strive to build peace, a desire for peace, a willingness to work for peace in the hearts and minds of all of our people. I believe that we can.
-John F. Kennedy (cited in Stockland, 2008, p. 77)

The future belongs to those who believe in the beauty of their dreams.
-Eleanor Roosevelt (cited in Schlup & Whisenhunt, 2001, p. 2)

To reach peace, teach peace.
-Pope John Paul II (1979)

Re-Viewing Pedagogical Possibility and Praxis

In picturing peace, and re-picturing peace, in their own lives, these education students not only began to conceptualize peace more fully and deeply, and as experientially attentive, but from such were able to work from these emerging understandings to consider afresh what teaching for peace might actually mean. Only 60% of these prospective teachers, however, actually addressed the pedagogical implications issuing from their inquiries into peace as imagined and lived; additionally, those who did attended largely to broad areas of address rather than explicating particular pedagogical strategies for promoting peace—a "finding" that surprised me, especially given my experience of pre-service teachers' affinities for and anxieties about identifying and knowing specific instructional strategies. A possible explanation for this outcome may be found practically in the fact that perhaps a good deal, too much, was asked of education students via this one assignment, especially as documented in written form in but one to two pages, such that presenting the meanings of images taken and reflections upon them respecting peace, as well as upon the process of inquiry, left little room for additionally engaging implications for teaching.

Perhaps also, education students may have benefited from modeling and support in analyzing images and meanings generated, and
insights taken from the process; and then brainstorming pedagogical
possibilities, gleaning pedagogical insights, and considering specific
teaching implications from such analysis. Another reason may be that
some participants expressed a realization that peace perhaps had
different meanings for and was experienced differently by different
people—or for and by themselves even at different times—and was
largely dependent on memory, aspiration, experience, and context.
Thus, perhaps some prospective teachers felt that pedagogy for peace
could only be subjectively created in the particular classroom context
in which one was teaching; or that apart from the actual children,
curriculum, and context, only general principles or directions or
broad issues or topics could be considered.

Still, as highlighted above, more than 80% of participants did include some discussion of their own learning through this inquiry, and
of their approach to and process of inquiry—such were ripe with
pedagogical insight too; and with that which was articulated explicitly in relation to implications for teaching for peace provided a number of promising directions for further inquiry, as well as for
potentially re-imagining, renewing, and realizing our dreams of
peace. The project itself seemed, as well, to cultivate or at least support an orientation to peace in these prospective teachers that embraced meaningfully both ethics and desire, and in an integral and
complementary rather than oppositional way. From this substance,
thus, three broad ideas emerged through my analysis and interpretation in relation to pedagogies for peace: (1) a peaceful teacher present
to and with students, (2) a relational (intersubjectivity-centered)
curriculum grounded in context and community, and (3) an explicit
design for teaching peace and enacting peace practices.

Teach Who You Are/Be Peace With Students

I choose doggedly to pursue peace. A teacher must make a conscientious effort to pursue peace. (Celia, 4/19/07)

The "beginning with me" of peace was a theme that emerged strongly in relation to the work of teaching peace. Prospective teachers spoke of the need to intentionally seek to embody and pursue peace for oneself if one were ever to hope to teach it to others. Some who were student teaching at the time of this "picturing peace" query affirmed as well that this choice must be made daily, ongoingly, described as a struggle, too, in the context of life in elementary and middle-school classrooms. Others highlighted the significance of knowing self, finding one's own balance and way to peace, setting personal peace goals, going within, and opening up the self to surprises and possibilities.

Many spoke of children themselves as the source not only of such surprise and possibility, but also of peace, as vehicles of peace, as well. In this, the task of teachers, too, was not only to inspire children to peace through their own lived example as role models, but also to learn peace from children, to observe and study children to learn peace, and also what peace may mean for each child. A few education students highlighted the fact that what is peace for him or her as teacher may not be optimal for all children, pointing to the import of getting to know each child personally as a teacher as much as possible, and from such, creating curricula and learning opportunities that are inclusive of peace practices for each and for all. As such, curriculum design and teaching practice are drawn from the lives and loves of children—personal expression and empowerment deemed important overarching goals for each student, involving self-reflection and awareness, as well as both teacher and student finding what each loves and enjoys doing, and ways to do and engage such in the work of teaching and learning. Of course, the with-ness here, in terms of being ("peace") with students, was ever present in prospective teachers' insights into peace pedagogy too.

Community as Curriculum and Person-Centered Pedagogy

Thus, affirming the with-ness, much of what was pedagogically outlined reflecting picturing peace as teachers were possibilities pointing to what I might call a "curriculum of connection" or "community as curriculum"—engaging explicitly and implicitly teaching certain values and attitudes and dispositions, and cultivating a sense of classroom community. Such meant, for the teacher, developing and establishing an environment in which there was authentic care, respect, and love for each other—among students as well as between teacher and student. In such a place, community members would be encouraged and taught to admit mistakes, support each other, embrace each other fondly, and accept, appreciate, and celebrate differences. Teresa (4/19/07), an education student who was particularly struck with how deeply implicated in peace for her were her past experiences and memories, was critical of the disconnected ways by which educators typically seek to engage children with curriculum, as well as with each other, alluding also to the importance of meaningfully connecting past with present, and both with future aspiration and agency too:

> If students' culture, language, and background are not represented in the...classes we teach, how can they ever make the connections between themselves and what they can do to bring about a more peaceful world? Perhaps if everybody took more time to embrace peace through our connections to the past, we would be fresher to use what we have experienced, felt, and learned to how we personally can contribute to overcome inequality in our world and help educate students to do the same.

Prospective teachers spoke of instilling the values and dispositions of tolerance and appreciation of diversity, individuality, and independence as well as community, collective inquiry, dialogue, and reflection. A few prospective teachers spoke of the importance of freedom and choice within structure—shared rules supportive of harmonious, artful classroom life. A number of these education students also emphasized the import of sharing oneself with others, and listening to others—coming to truly know one another through conversation, sharing, and talking; students with each other and among themselves; teacher, as a community member too, with student, and students. Again, self-reflection and responsibility became important for all—realizing how one reacts and responds to others, as well as the impact of such, and of one's actions, on them. Working and playing together, engaging difference concurrently with a sense of unity and we-ness or with-ness was also pedagogically emphasized by prospective teachers. Chloe (4/20/07), who loves photography and was also student teaching at the time, brought this love to her teaching to create a shared experience for/with her students; describing this specific curricular example in her writing, she reflects:

> I gave students in my third grade student teaching placement a disposable camera and asked them to take pictures. Each child made his or her own decision what to shoot. The results were splendid and the images were passed around and discussed. Through these pictures, these children were able to share information about themselves and what they enjoyed doing, as well as about their families, their backgrounds, their cultures, their neighborhoods. It was a unifying experience, which enhanced the sense of community in our classroom. I intend to bring photography into the classroom again. It can do remarkable things.

Teaching Peace, Actually, and Practices for Peace

While no other participants reported actually engaging students similarly in such "picturing peace" or pursuit of peace inquiries, many of them affirmed the role of teaching inquiry and cultivating curiosity in relation to pedagogy for peace, and also at least 40% of all participants (two-thirds of the 60% who explicitly addressed pedagogical possibilities for promoting peace) endorsed actually engaging students in the "picturing peace" assignment they had undertaken for our class. Several prospective teachers explicitly spoke more broadly, as well, of intentionally teaching peace, via the development of peace curricula, built in large measure, too, from students' views of peace, based on inquiries into peace in their own lives. A number of goals were linked to such student research, as well, for example: the realization that peace is all around, ever-present and available, when one takes the time to notice, and look; and that the meaning of peace differs for each individual, largely shaped by individual circumstances and experiences, such that peace, and ideas about it, must be shared for insight into peace and promoting it.

Relatedly, a few participants highlighted the invaluable role that "view-changing" activities, like this one and others, could play in this work. Katie (4/24/06) explains: "One of the most powerful pieces of this project was that it helped me to remember the power of looking at things differently. No matter how many times you've seen something, you can *see* it differently, no matter how trite that sounds." Herein, cultivating in students the ability to shift perspective on the world was pedagogically posited, as well as simply exposing students to the world's richness and beauty, including the city's "magic" and cultural diversity, and the variety afforded through a multicultural curriculum. Through this kind of engagement with the world, some prospective teachers also suggested embracing the work of attending to the cycles of life and of nature, and realizing and appreciating life's ineffable vibrancy.

> Ironically, it was the Europeans who landed in America who wanted peace, and they who disrupted their own peace by bringing over slaves from America. Peace is something that I feel exists until it is disrupted. (Eva, 4/20/07)

In the same vein, too, many of these education students wrote of teaching peace as it relates to war, injustice, and oppression. Most were mindful of the requirement of a certain balance here in juxtaposing presentations of peace and its absence, and grounding such work in a sense of hope and agency: studying the goodness and humanity still present amid the horrors of human history, experiences of joy and beauty even amid suffering and tragedy, and initiatives for and achievements of peace as well as those situations and places in great want of peace or wherein peace is yet a distant hope. A few students here advocated the search for and teaching of positive peace stories of inspiration and hope—for example, through the life of Gandhi or Susan B. Anthony, or the work of the civil rights movement or Jonas Salk's invention of the polio vaccine—emphasizing the importance of giving students real role models of and for peace from which to learn and follow. The study of current events also became a focal point for more fully engaging students in the world of which they are a part, and partly responsible. The manner in which such should be taken up was important to prospective teachers too—books more than just words, history more than just dates, and curricula made meaningful and relatable to learners; but some of those aspects expressly mentioned for consideration.

Thus, pedagogical implications outlined also included offering students the personal tools needed to handle unfair conditions in their own lives, like problem-solving and conflict-resolution skills—whatever might assist children in learning to faithfully attend to their own hurts, forgive acts of betrayal, and resolve differences in the course of living, for example. From the space and place of their own lives, then, students could be encouraged to engage in meaningful collective work—which may differ for each child—addressing particular efforts for justice and peace; like protecting the environment by working to reduce litter, noise, and pollution or participating in demonstrations against war.

Through these broad strokes and particular practices, prospective teachers ultimately suggested that children, too, could be intentionally and explicitly taught to reflect upon, dream, and practice peace; to pursue peace "doggedly"—whether via age-appropriate meditation practices, as proposed also by some, or inquiring into what is common among them respecting peace and building and nurturing such together in collective labor, as endorsed by others—in the face of adversity, embracing perseverance and hard work, as responsible and responsive world citizens. Herein, too, all seemed to affirm the humanity and agency of children; the languages of desire and of ethics, yet mostly of hope, in relation to them and to their work with them as teachers; and reflection and practice toward, more aptly, a praxis of possibility, in their pursuits of pedagogies for and of peace—all of which, in and of themselves, may work to further renewal of our dreams of peace and their realization.

Re-Voicing Pedagogical Possibility and Praxis

In the spring of 2011, during the course of this study, three former education students in two different settings in New York City, now teachers, afforded me the opportunity,[1] to gain a small window into their intentional and explicit pursuits with their own elementary students respecting pedagogical possibility and praxis for re-viewing and re-voicing peace—and thus, for the renewal of our dreams of peace and their realization. In offering here brief portraits of and reflections on these lived examples, I hope not only to illustrate something of what such insights into and ideas for teaching for peace might actually look like—and perhaps effect—in practice, but also to extend such re-viewing and re-voicing, in the sense that not only do these teachers design and enact curricula in particular contexts, and through the lenses of their own visions and voices concerning peace, but also *with* their own particular students, who bring who they are and what they know of and hope for peace, too, to such work.

I highlight, as well, herein—via this section heading—the notion of voice, as these new teachers engaged and affirmed their own agency in articulating and actualizing their own pedagogies for peace, from the sites of their own subjectivities, in conditions of standardization offering little support for such; and this also, in foregrounding the agency and voice of their students, each intent upon empowering students to address obstacles to peace and adopt peace practices in their own lives, as well as for their schools, communities, and world. The first example presents a peace curriculum in a first-grade classroom in a charter school in East Harlem[2]; the second, an inquiry into violence in a fourth-grade classroom in the South Bronx.

---

1 I am greatly indebted to my colleague, Dr. Debbie Sonu, who—from her interests in exploring how elementary teachers navigate critical issues in social studies involving peace and violence with students, as well as young children's thoughts about peace and violence—recruited me to this work in New York City schools with elementary teachers and students, through a grant she procured at Hunter College. Her initiative, then, was generative of my reconnecting with these former education students, NYC teachers, and our joint participations in this larger study. In this, I also enjoyed the opportunity to speak with them about peace, and violence, and their educational engagements with their own students around these concerns, in their classrooms; observing and working with and speaking with their students as well.
2 The names of former students, featured teachers, as well as the schools in which they are working, have been changed to protect their anonymity.

"Take time to practice peacemaking."/ "Work up your toolbox for peace."[3]

Believe Charter School in East Harlem is located adjacent to—one could say in the community of—public housing projects, in a building it also shares with other elementary schools. I am hurriedly making my way on an early morning in early May, my first visit there being as a visiting presenter for a school-wide hosted "Career Day." Here, I will talk to two classrooms of first-graders—the "Stars" and "Comets" classes—about becoming and being a professor, and answer questions they have about my vocation. Ruth and Derrick, former students of mine, are co-teachers in one of these classrooms, and responsible for my presence at this event.

In this context, I am registering little, sadly, about the character of the neighborhood or community—but for a few enticing opportunities I note for Spanish, Mexican, and Cuban cuisine amid a surprising number of posh nouveau-American restaurants and bars, foodie that I am—or the school environment, at least initially: focused on arriving on time, getting to where I need to go, and engaging well with students in their interests and wonderings about the work of being a professor. I remember the morning, though, as fresh and dewy, the well-manicured lawns and trees—park-like areas—among the buildings in this housing complex, and the excited welcome with which I am met by the coordinator of Career Day, who leads me to a lovely breakfast spread before which are gathered parents and event participants, where the principal also greets us warmly. We are also given Believe t-shirts, and I find that everyone in the school is sporting the tees as well, though in different colors by different school grades. Herein, I sense a spirited and positive environment, of clean appearance, where student work is celebrated, proudly posted throughout the school; and also note an emphasis on literacy in classrooms, via bulletin boards and posters.

Apart from being made well aware of my inability to compete with the popularity of a young man on the career panel with me who works on the Broadway production of *The Lion King*, I remember

---

3 This heading comes from the ideas expressed by these two co-teachers—former students—Ruth and Derrick, and quoted in that order, in an interview on June 21, 2011.

most upon this first visit my surprise at the striking difference between the two first-grade classes; and this, despite similar conversations and management strategies engaged via counting and clapping
and movement—a kind of "call and response" curriculum enacted in
the way of engaging collective attention and participation, and
ensuring smooth progress in moving through designed educational
objectives and experiences. What I am struck by is a profound felt
difference in the tenor of each classroom; and regarding this use of
clapping, counting, and call and response.

I am reminded of just how influential the teacher can be and often
is in establishing the mode and manner of being and relating in a
classroom, and the impact of such upon all that is educationally
embraced and taken up therein. Here, I wonder if the particular
commitments of Ruth and Derrick, in fact, to teaching peace account
in some substantial measure for the differences discerned. In their
class, the students seem not only to direct the discussion, positing
their own authentic questions to Career Day participants—in contrast
to those in the other classroom—but also demonstrate a marked
capacity for identifying points of affirmation and articulating such
appreciations to us. The event concludes with a signature collective
practice of "wiggling their fingers" in our direction, by which they
hope to send us their "quiet love" as well as thanks. I also received
handmade thank-you cards from these students shortly after this
visit, elucidating particulars on what each child learned and especially liked about my job, with illustrations, much to my surprise and
delight.

Perhaps, though, I should not have been at all surprised. My
initial, more formal, observation in the classroom of Ruth and Derrick
shortly thereafter reveals a context in which such thoughtfulness and
kindness, and "real-world" curriculum, is actively cultivated and
nurtured, and something of the norm in this classroom. Rather than
the typically posted class rules or constitution, this group has co-
created their "Community Promises"; upon the walls are also found
visible reminders of key tenets for harmonious relations and successful conflict resolution, via an emphasis on each classroom community
member as a "peacemaker": that is, peacemakers use I statements and
share appreciations. Additionally, the classroom houses a unique

specially designed space known as the "peace corner" to which I was immediately drawn upon first entering the room. I noticed an inviting and interesting collection of materials therein: pillows and plants; paper and writing and art supplies; artfully crafted visuals with charts outlining possibilities for making peaceful choices; a diverse selection of picture books on peace and peacemaking and of inspiring individuals like Anne Frank, Ruby Bridges, Gandhi, Sadako Sasaki, Martin Luther King, Jr., and Barack Obama; and even a timer to support intentional retreat, and focus on counting and breathing as methods for calming down.

Later, I learned that the peace corner was created to empower students to manage their own emotions and behaviors in life-affirming and nonviolent ways, and solve their own conflicts as self-affirmed and cultivated peacemakers. Through this structure, a student is able to choose time alone in a safe place as needed, during the course of the day in authentic moments of frustration or distress, to not only feel his or her feelings, but also adopt peaceful choices for expressing such feelings and attending to the situations accompanying them. Subsequent observations revealed students taking advantage of this space—reading, drawing, writing, breathing, and even punching pillows. Relatedly, I noticed students with peacemaker "choice rings," that suggested choices such as counting to ten or asking nicely, and highlighted the idea of going to the peace corner, when needed.

In fact, on one of my early visits in this—what I found to be—loving and playful community, educationally rich classroom, and lively and ordered environment—I witnessed a rather remarkable engagement with and in the peace corner. The first-grade students had just concluded an enjoyable and participatory period in which small groups practiced readers' theater pieces of selected folktales, which they then presented to and discussed with the entire class on the large rug. I was especially delighted here to participate with a small group exploring *Pinocchio*; and to look on as students performed for their peers, and their enthusiastic teachers had them all dramatically work to embody their characters—whether animal or plant or human—with sound, movement, and gesture, as well as retell storylines in their own words. As Derrick directed students in

finishing up this learning activity and preparing to leave the classroom for recess, a third-grade girl entered the classroom and asked
Ruth if she could spend some time in the peace corner.

Apparently, the peace corner had become known throughout the
school and was utilized by some of the teachers, and students, in
other classes in times of need, as well. Raechelle, this third-grader,
reported that she had kicked her "enemy." After spending about five
minutes in the peace corner by herself, Raechelle asked to speak with
Ruth, to tell her story. She had been reading from a picture book
about Martin Luther King, Jr.'s "big words" and found a passage that
spoke to her and helped her, which she also wanted to read and
share: "Love can solve the problems of the world." Prompted by their
discussion and Ruth's questions— "Is it easy to love your enemies?"
and "How could you love your enemy here?"—Raechelle decided to
make her "enemy" a gift, an artful card that presented this wisdom
from King inside, and hearts, and a written apology: "I just didn't
want to be touched then. You are so good to me and I am not to you. I
am sorry." When Raechelle decided she was ready to go back to her
classroom, she was smiling and talking about making enemies into
friends.

The peace corner, too, is but one reflection of the ways in which
Ruth and Derrick seek to actively teach peace to their students,
having intentionally developed a peace curriculum, directly taught,
and infused into the structure of living and learning together in the
classroom, and in community. Such includes, among other things:
introducing students to key historical and public figures of peace and
working with them to adopt particular "peace practices" these figures
inspire; teaching, modeling, and practicing with children conflict
resolution and problem-solving skills; promoting "apologies of
meaning"—beyond simply saying "I'm sorry"—and "I" messages,
through which a child takes responsibility for and owns his or her
own ideas, feelings and actions; and establishing a community
practice of giving appreciations that compel class members to look for
the good in others and express gratitude openly.

This peace curriculum also involves creating peacemaker puppets
for use in role-playing harmonious, affirming relations, particularly to
work through moments of conflict in the midst of a circle of friends

who can offer ideas for resolution; initiating the "peace patrol," through which rotating helpers assist friends in their peacemaking efforts and in solving conflicts; participating in meditation, guided imagery, and yoga practice; and engaging children in the recognition, expression, and articulation of their feelings via charades, writing, or drawing. For example, one morning, each student took a "journey" through the mind's eye in a big purple balloon to meet up with a friend in the destination of his or her choice. This generated lively conversation and a spirit of joy—and transformed a scene of agitation from some prior classroom conflict. The tenor of relations I felt as a visitor in this classroom over the last two months of the school year attested, in this way, to the success of their curriculum: students are affectionate with and kind to each other; enthusiastically taking up their identities as peacemakers, it seems, they are quick to help each other, share supplies, and offer one another encouraging and uplifting words.

Alas, however, I learn that with a new principal, and pressures mounting in relation particularly to student achievement as measured via high-stakes, standardized test scores, the peace curriculum so carefully created by Ruth and Derrick is being squeezed out in mandates to spend more time on determined literacy and math skills. In fact, the principal has expressed concern about the peace corner, uncomfortable with the idea of children having choices about withdrawing briefly from classroom instructional activities for any reason whatsoever. In my meeting with her, as well, I noted her emphasis on rigorous academics, high expectations, and students achieving mastery of learning standards, which, while not necessarily at odd with aims relating to peace, seemed to dominate our discussion to the exclusion of much else. Her perspective mirrors in part, as well, the mission of the school, particularly as articulated through a rather dismal portrayal of the context in which the school resides and to which it is expressly seeking to respond.

As a community-based public charter school, the Believe website frames the school's mission to promote student achievement and potential in relation to some grim East Harlem statistics: an area possessed of many of the lowest-performing New York City schools, fewer than half of all elementary students here meet the reading standards for the city and state, and fewer than half of all adults achieve a high school diploma; the majority of families live in poverty, and the community is known to have the city's highest rates of childhood obesity, asthma, and diabetes as well. Thus, the school has a full-time social worker and guidance counselor on site; stresses mastery of state-sanctioned learning standards, albeit in a nurturing environment attentive to the emotional, physical, social, as well as intellectual needs of its students; offers extended-day and -year programs; and embraces an inclusion model of co-teaching teams in each classroom affording a 12:1 student to teacher ratio, supportive of special education, English as a second language, and cultural difference, as well.

The portrait of duress, of course, in many ways belies the cultural wealth of this largely Hispanic, Latino/a and Black neighborhood, as well as the gentrification already well underway there. Nonetheless, the school's demographics (as reported: 61% Hispanic, 30% Black, 3% Asian, and 0% White) do reflect the poverty outlined therein in that 83% of its 200 students qualify for free lunch. Interestingly, as well, in interviews with Ruth and Derrick, I discovered that the peace curriculum was initially designed and taught the year before in response to the anger, turmoil, and aggressive behavior displayed by so many of the children in that class—in contrast to the young boys and girls I met each week in class, full of smiles and laughs and warm greetings—and more so perhaps than the personal and professional commitments of these educators as they undertook their first years of teaching. Ruth (6/21/11) explains:

> ...last year, our peace curriculum was a direct response to the emotional difficulties that our kids were having—like tearing up the room and wanting to die and stuff like that. We were really focusing on strategies for inner peace. So all these peacemaker superheroes served as role models for how people can find inner peace when the world around them is just a nightmare.... this year, totally different, more about social conflicts and resolutions...

In this way, the pedagogies for peace taken to and up in this first-grade class reflected something of the subjectivities of the students as well as those of these teachers. Both Ruth and Derrick do, however, articulate explicit commitments to educational work aimed at social justice and peace, and have intentionally chosen to work with low-income and *minoritized*[4] populations as teachers in concert with such commitments. Both also locate the origins of these interests within their own histories and experiences, not essentially or wholly emerging from their present teaching practice or engagement with students.

A relatively slight and small woman in her thirties with wavy brown hair, sparkling eyes, and a charming smile, Ruth's gentleness and genuineness are somehow equally matched with her charisma and passion. Concerning the origins of her understandings of and interests in peace, she narrates a story quite consciously that began in her youth and led directly to her ideas of teaching peace:

> My whole childhood was about the Middle East conflict because my dad is Israeli. So that was just kind of a part of my daily life and the news and the questions and all the debate. When I got to college...all my liberal friends somehow were the opposite of what I'd been hearing all my life from my dad and my grandpa and my grandma. So I have spent a lot of time thinking about the Middle East conflict and the one solution that I came up with was crop dusting and yoga. I thought to myself, something has to happen in the school and in children to create a sense of calm. This is a hot desert place with only one fresh water source. People are getting all these different messages all the time....horrific images, and...I just see all this heat and something needs to happen to cool it down. That cool down has to happen in individuals. It's not going to happen in the government. It's not going to happen on any large scale, so it got me thinking there has to be a way to educate starting really young how people can be content—find ways to be peaceful in their own lives so that they don't have all this anger at all these external forces and larger systems that they cannot control.

Interestingly, Derrick—a native New Yorker, and educated in city public and public charter schools—credits his middle-school teachers with igniting in him a passion for peace, and for teaching it. He explains: "My school was focused around teaching tolerance and social advocacy and from there I felt empowered to, kind of, bring about change, and that is what led me to teaching" (6/21/11). He highlights the ways in which he remembers his teachers guiding the

---

4 Unsure exactly where to locate the use of this term, I believe I first heard it from my colleague, Dr. Debbie Sonu, referencing the marginalization that largely and systemically occurs for students at the intersections of race and class, particularly to those identified as low-income or in poverty and "of color."

students in deconstructing texts, talking seriously about social issues, and critically looking at the world in which they lived; and elaborates further on this influence, as he joined political groups, learned mediation and debate, and got involved in protests against particular injustices.

Though he might protest such a description, as I interact with him in his classroom, with his dark black hair and skin, towering stature, and welcoming and warm presence, this man in his mid-twenties is something like a big teddy bear, an affectionate father figure, especially among his little first-graders—bold, comforting, and protective. For Derrick, pursuing peace in the classroom with his students means, then, attending well to issues that arise, like bullying, or things that have students worried, in and out of school; and communicating and seeking solutions. His views on peace reflect such pursuits, and in relation to the earlier life influences of which he has spoken: nonviolence, movement toward social justice and positive change, labor to correct wrongs and systematic and historically rooted cycles of injustice. Of his own pursuits and promotions of peace with students, he concludes: "We need to take time to practice peacemaking…. If not, it won't happen" (6/21/11).

In our conversation, Ruth (6/21/11) concurs—"you need to spend time, work up your toolbox for peace"—and adds that such practice involves conscious effort and often in the face of challenge; she also talks about her work on her own peacemaking skills in the face of reactive family members, while seeking to teach them to children. Yet, these teachers expressed a confidence that if children are taught to live and love peace, they too will consciously choose it, advocate for it, and pass peace along. The two speak fondly of moments when they hear the children encouraging each other to "give peace" to a flower or take delight in rescuing a bug from harm and return it to its outside home, or take time to breathe while taking a test. Ruth (6/21/11) remembers that during a fieldtrip hike the class was taking, when they found a turtle on a rock, one of the girls asked: "Is a turtle a peacemaker?" She had noticed how quiet and calm the creature seemed. Then, Ruth defines peace actually as inspired by another one of her students, Gizelle. This young girl stood up in "church" on their field trip to a play village and proclaimed:

"Peace is a culture of respect for each other and the earth." When she said
that, this light bulb went off in my head. Wow! That is the best definition I
have ever heard.

Learning "peace" from their own first-graders, perhaps Ruth and
Derrick have succeeded indeed in their pedagogical efforts to pass
peacemaking along.

"That your questions are worth something is big"[5]

On a warm afternoon in May, I made my first visit to P.S. 1722 in the
South Bronx. The neighborhood, much like many others I have
known in New York City, was bustling with activity as I exited the
subway. Vendors could be found on the sidewalk selling fresh
mangos and refreshing fruit ices; sales were advertised by stores
lining the streets, many open air, with wares positioned strategically
in front of shops, and men young and old could be found gathered
together in various ways conversing. Women pushed strollers and
toted toddlers as well. Crowded, urban, this area of the South Bronx,
amid heat and concrete, showcased still some green trees and lawns,
and a park was also happily situated across from the school. Signs of
wear and some disrepair—empty boarded-up lots, spray-painted
obscenities, strewn trash—could also be found, albeit amid scaffolding in front of the school, for example, signifying the work of upkeep
and repair. Some such sights differentiated this place, for me, from
my own former residential Brooklyn neighborhood, and that of the
university where I work on the Upper West Side—actually traditionally a part of Harlem, but in present times afforded the lovely name of
Morningside Heights.

Additionally, the faces I met on my way to P.S. 1722, and within
the school, as well—apart from the teachers and many other school
employees—were largely brown and black, in contrast to my own
white complexion, and the more diversified palette encountered
where I lived in Brooklyn and work in Harlem. The 500-plus students

---

5 This heading comes directly from words spoken by teacher and former student
Dorothy, in an interview on June 24, 2011—whose peace thought and pedagogy are
featured in the following section.

attending P.S.1722, from prekindergarten through fifth grades, reflect the demographics of their community: 73% are identified as Hispanic, 23% as Black and 1% as White; and 94% of them qualify for free lunch. Many of their teachers, however, are not members of this community, and Dorothy—my former student now teaching there—reports that she and others typically commute there to teach and meet other professional responsibilities, but do not spend much additional time in the area—some attention given, as well, to leaving the area before dark. Still, here, in the afternoon, one senses little of such misgivings or forebodings; clearly amid others in a place many call home, with all the markers of life fully lived via work and play vividly displayed.

In fact, as I entered the school, I was first struck by how beautiful and well maintained the building was, in addition to the friendly welcome of the security guard receiving visitors. As the exterior, obscured by scaffolding, shows signs of being actively cared for and attended, one notices the sight, and smell, of fresh paint in pleasant colors throughout the interior, and the artful ironwork around the stairwell. The word "peace" in many different languages is also painted along the walls, along with uplifting sayings in the halls, showcasing the works and ideas of figures like Martin Luther King, Jr. and Maya Angelo—alongside student work posted on bulletin boards throughout as well. The classrooms enjoy large windows and high ceilings, similarly well ordered and welcoming. Most class-rooms, though, are not air-conditioned, making for much discomfort on hot days in the city, and a lack of supplies and resources are also reported generally to be of much concern as well.

I am visiting what folks in the school call "the inquiry room," cen-tral to a school-wide effort to engage students in active inquiry around questions that matter to them, issuing from their own lives in their own communities. Dorothy, while working with a male teacher in her own ICT (integrated co-teaching) fourth-grade classroom, has taken leadership in guiding students' work in the inquiry class, collaborating enthusiastically with the director of the inquiry work for the school, also a teacher, and graduate of another program at Teachers College—Maria, a young Hispanic woman and literacy specialist who has been working at the school for some years now. In fact, the passion of these two young women for these endeavors has led them to co-present on such work at local and national conferences, and to begin writing about their inquiry curriculum and pedagogy, and their experiences with these students and others, for publication.

The inquiry room is organized well for exploration and research: varied and sundry materials are visibly showcased and accessible to students; different work areas have been set up to cultivate engagements of many kinds—for computer use, conversation and dialogue, study of documents, visual presentation of questions and findings. The class meets daily for an hour in the afternoon, some of this time drawn from extended day such that some students leave 20–25 minutes early during school dismissal. Students were working in groups during this visit. Their inquiry is directed toward understanding why their neighborhood is so violent. Charts and other graphic organizers are on the wall by which the students are conceptually mapping out their questions and lines of inquiry, thoughts, and findings in the course of working, and as tools for reflection and further inquiry. Of note to me on this day were key words and ideas recorded, such as gender, race, power, class, unfairness, rights violated, and cycle.

Today students are looking at newspapers and other forms of media news in groups—one pair, reading about a rape case; a larger group engaged with Maria discussing the role gender plays in the problem of violence. Dorothy is assisting others on the computer— attending searches and recording thoughts—but here and now, issues with the technology are absorbing much of the work time. Some students are more interested in our presence in the classroom—I am working here with a colleague and research partner—than the inquiry activities, in part due to this being our initial visit to the classroom. Jason[6]—a small, thin, friendly boy with fair skin, light-brown hair, and big green eyes—approaches me; aware that I am interested in their study, he decides to volunteer these thoughts: that the best response to violence is to run and hide (in the closet, with a phone).

---

6 The names of all elementary students used herein have been changed to protect their anonymity.

Many of the students seem to be engaged in the tasks at hand, albeit there is a fluid back and forth with on-task talk and behavior, and what might be considered off-task. The fact that this class is positioned at the end of the day may contribute to this case, as well as something of the nature of collective inquiry itself reflected herein— emergent, requiring flexibility, and conversation. John—a wiry and small albeit fierce and articulate Black student of notable reputation as a bully and troublemaker—wants to show me what he has written and drawn in his inquiry journal; he tells me that as a part of their inquiry work, they interviewed police officers who said that boys were more violent than girls or that they were picked up for violent charges more often. John then adds this commentary: "It's not fair." When I try to ask what he means exactly by this response, he leaves me and returns to his group's inquiry work.

This portrait of the inquiry classroom at work is somewhat typical, based on my observations during six or so visits to the school. What is perhaps not as visible as could be, especially as so powerfully constitutive of this scene, is something of its larger context. Dorothy's—and Maria's—fourth-graders represent a traditionally underserved and underachieving population: low-income and minoritized, most of these students are below grade level in reading and math, and 12 of the 22 students (11 boys and 11 girls) qualify for special education services, their education directed via Individual Education Plans (IEPs). Most of them are of Latino/a background—families largely from the Dominican Republic, Puerto Rico, or Mexico—or of African or African American descent, and a few are English Language Learners (ELLs)—and are Spanish speakers. While the academic competencies of the neighborhood residents are underdeveloped, these students are often described as "street smart," creative, and friendly.

In addition, in a national scene enforcing curriculum standardization, and this oriented around high-stakes testing, and a local one in which the school risks state sanctions as a failing school, it is unique for such an inquiry class as this one to even exist as much as persist— largely due to the vision of the principal, who herself once worked with lower-elementary children around inquiry through play to fruitful effect and has written about such. The inquiry approach also fits well within the school's express mission: to promote independence, confidence, academic achievement, and social responsibility in its children, via differentiated curriculum issuing from student needs, interests, and ideas; and to build partnerships with families and the community in designing the school around "transformative learning" in an inclusive environment wherein students are inspired to address problems in the world and seek to redress them.

Still, it is the teachers—most of them White, deemed among the best educated in the city, and committed to working with underserved populations—these in particular, who bring to this vision a strong critical lens, and heart for the aims of social justice and peace via education, which they seek also to enact via their curriculum and pedagogy; and such, in a context of much pressure and stress generated by troubling student and school scores.

Dorothy embraced this work, in this context, as a first-year teacher and the special educator on record, for her fourth-grade class—one that, by all accounts, was identified as highly challenging. The inquiry class offered her not only a mentor of sorts, and kindred educator, in Maria; but also a home for attending her hopes of addressing issues of social justice and peace with students, interests she reports were influenced much by her studies at Teachers College, as well as her encounters there and before with the works of Paulo Freire and relatedly those of Augusto Boal, from her college studies in theater. Principally, regarding her own work as a teacher, she was inspired by Freire's emphasis on the role of education as critical to the work of humanization, countering oppression, and cultivating human agency and freedom through problem posing, praxis—reflective action, and dialogue; and Boal's engagement with theater and the arts toward such purposes; she also felt that she could freely bring these ideas to the design of the inquiry class; as generally conceived and carried out, it was quite consistent with such. For students, she adds: "That your questions are worth something is big" (6/24/11).

Maria had been central to the birth of the inquiry room, and classes for each grade, at the school, in directing it framed through the work of critical literacy, to which she was most committed, a tradition greatly influenced also by the work of Freire and his pedagogy of critically "reading the word and the world" for greater awareness and agency in the world; empowered by such, too, to transform it.

The teachers thus initiated an inquiry cycle that Maria created in which students: (1) observe issues/topics pertaining to their lives/communities, (2) develop questions based on these observations, (3) conduct research and explore the issue or topic through multiple sign systems (for example, drama, art, writing, technology), and (4) respond to findings through some sort of social action. The actual process was articulated through three key terms: Recognize, Understand, and Act. For this particular class, this particular year, student work revolved around their question: What causes the violence in our neighborhood?

"I observed—through full-class, small-group, lunch time, playground, conversation—my students talking a lot about the violence in their neighborhood," Dorothy (6/24/11) reports. In this way, her own commitment to watching and listening to her students closely as central to enacting responsive pedagogy, and leadership in the inquiry work with her students, seems to have strongly influenced the question the class actually settled on for the subject of their yearlong study. Interestingly, as well, in speaking with her further, here her descriptions of peace and of teaching it are articulated in some measure in terms of violence—that is, the freedom and security known and lived in its absence, or in deliverance from it.

> I feel like a peaceful world is definitely where people are not afraid to do something, to either speak or just be: if you are feeling threatened by something, it's never a good feeling. The absence of that can lift a huge load off your shoulders. (6/24/11)

She both desires peace for herself and her students, and feels a responsibility to pursue it for herself and her students, as well, perhaps in response to contexts and experiences wanting peace—past and present.

Dorothy, in many ways, could not be more different from most of her students. Twenty-six, tall, and thin, with long blonde hair and big green eyes, she grew up in a Pennsylvania village town, and attended a private religious school, one also where peace was much spoken of and advocated; from an upper-middle-class family of six, both

parents earned advanced degrees, and afforded her what she describes as a sheltered, if not privileged, childhood. Still, Dorothy
shares with her students a concern about violence, and the ways in
which even the threat of it violates peace and freedom and joy; she
frames her discussion with me around two key vignettes. In the first,
she speaks about her college years in Washington, DC, in which she
often felt scared, and how awful it was living abidingly with such a
feeling.

> I remember being on the subway and a bunch of guys came up to me, and I
> remember…[one of them saying]: "I am going to fucking shoot you in the
> head and don't think I won't fucking blow this place up." I think it was my
> freshman year and I'd never had a situation like that before…. for four years
> on I looked in the Metro car to see who was in there before I got on.
> (6/24/11)

In the second story, she speaks of a recent experience as a mugging victim. After this incident, in which she was not hurt but her cell
phone was stolen, she says she forced herself to take the same route to
the subway, even though she wanted to avoid it—partly because she
was "pissed" and not going to let "this teenage boy" who had perpe-
trated the theft take her power away from her. Generally, upon
moving to New York from DC, she reports having felt a huge release,
so much safer, and even despite this crime—so much about one's
state of mind too, she reflects: "I think your mind is unbelievably
powerful" (6/24/11). Dorothy comments further how her principal
worried that the mugging had happened near the school, while in
actuality it had happened in the gentrified Brooklyn neighborhood
where she lived.

Even here, though, as a teacher Dorothy articulates a commitment
that she feels was not wholly present in her own education: genuine
engagement in addressing what is present, openly and honestly—
"whatever the children come in with." In this sense, even as her
experiences come to bear in strong ways in her educational work—in
what was felt to be absent or false as well as present therein; she
seems to suggest that teaching peace, or anything else for that matter,
must begin with the particular students with whom one is engaged—
their experiences, interests, needs, questions, in the present context
that is shared. Of course, this does not negate bringing oneself wholly

as a teacher, in one's singularity, to this endeavor as well. In this way, while there was in her religious education a somewhat predetermined explicit curriculum of sorts endorsing peace, as a teacher here, with these students, the curriculum emerges from student as well as teacher concerns and questions about violence—peace more implicitly or indirectly pursued perhaps as understanding is gleaned and responsive action sought in such study.

In the midst of this work of studying violence with her fourth-graders—expressing as a first-year teacher a strong sense of what she does not yet know about this work, the experimental and ever-falling-short way in which she feels she and Maria are undertaking this inquiry with these students—Dorothy highlights certain goals she feels are being attended herein whereby students are: drawing upon and together home/cultural/community and school knowledge to gain new knowledge about the world in which they live; practicing critical inquiry and higher-level thinking meaningfully in ways transferable to other contexts and conditions; and using multiple sign systems to make and express meaning. Specifically and principally, she noted that her students arrived at the concept of power via this inquiry: gleaning insight into the presence of power struggles in the dynamics that make for violence, the human desire for power, and the import of basic needs and vulnerability to violence ensuing when these are unmet. For herself, she continues: "I think the biggest thing that I wanted them to understand is that it was in their hands—whatever is out there, however their life is at the moment, is that they need to learn that it's 'you' ultimately... that...it can change. That it is always within 'you'" (6/24/11).

While the action piece collectively decided upon through this inquiry entailed the making of artistic works to be shared with other classes at the school, Dorothy can't help but feel, or hope at least, that the empowered response of some of her students to the suffering of children in Japan after the tsunami disaster has something to do with "peace" lessons learned through their inquiry into violence: A beautiful Latina student, Johanna, felt something had to be done, and directed the class, school, and community in putting on a bake sale: involving writing letters to parents, teachers, and students, asking them to donate, bake, buy, and sell; researching and deciding upon how and where to best send monies. Through her efforts, more than $600 was raised. "Johanna's bake sale was amazing—an example of the kids actually stepping up and doing something, and the way that they felt was probably the best that they felt all year" (6/21/11).

Herein, prospective teachers and a few "become" teachers have offered us insight into possibilities for teaching peace, via broad strokes and particular scenes—coming from the sites of their own subjectivities, experiences, and situations, and reflections upon them. In the least, I have attempted here to listen to these prospective teachers and practicing teachers, and learn peace, and pedagogy for peace, from and through them. In enjoying the opportunity, too, to view peace and pedagogies for peace, from the vantage point of my presence in these two classrooms, in the midst of children who were engaging such as well, I was also able to make "peace," as it were, with a few of them. I turn to this in the next chapter: seeking peace through the eyes of children.

Chapter 6
Seeking Peace through Children's Eyes

Seek the wisdom of the ages, but look at the world through the eyes of a child.   -Ron Wild (cited in McGlynn, 2011, p. 28)

Blessed be childhood, which brings down something of heaven into the midst of our rough earthliness.
                    -Henri Frederic Amiel (cited in Stowers, 1998, p. 13)

If we are to teach real peace in this world, and if we are to carry on a real war against war, we shall have to begin with the children.
                    -Mohandas Gandhi (cited in Macer & Saad-Zoy,
                    2010, p. 51)

While I began this work, in many ways, inspired by Gandhi's assertion that to claim and create peace for ourselves and our world we must begin with—perhaps learn *from* and *with*, in teaching—children, I had not initially planned to literally do so, as such, to work or play or converse directly with children for seeking and speaking peace anew, and pedagogically. I imagined my response to be consonant with, even requisite to, this claim, though, in inviting prospective teachers to picture peace in their own lives through fresh eyes, and reflect upon such experiential and lived depictions to consider anew not only possibilities for peace for themselves but also for teaching peace to and with children in their own classrooms. I still believe such a project is constitutive of and critical to this larger aspiration—especially given a context in which teachers, as those most intimately and intentionally educationally engaged with children (and by this, I mean in a more systematically concerted and collective manner than parents and family members), are increasingly constrained and controlled by political agendas aimed at "teaching by numbers" (Taubman, 2009) via standardized curriculum, high-stakes testing, and punitive policy in an audit and surveillance culture.

Education itself, as a project engaging the work of cultivating our humanity (Nussbaum, 1997), what Freire (1970/1993) calls our "historical vocation of humanization," requires the full and free presence—vision, agency, and voice—of, in the least, teachers and students, in dialogue, engaging and exploring together what it means to be human, and what might make for harmonious, fruitful, freeing, and fulfilling relations among us. Here, then, I am delighted that during the course of my own inquiry, through the generosity and inspiration of a few of my former students become teachers, I have been able to seek peace, in some small measure, through the eyes of at least a few children, as well. I hope, too, to showcase something of the light and insight gathered from such beholding. First, I offer by way of introduction an overview of the work undertaken with children concerning peace in these two New York City elementary classrooms, classrooms and contexts initially described in Chapter 5. Then, I present particular peace profiles I have thus far gleaned from the children in each classroom. Such an approach is meant neither to minimize the differences existing among children in each setting, nor marginalize the distinct voices of each child, but rather to highlight common emerging themes, and as potentially pertaining to the pedagogical peace projects undertaken by their teachers with them. In concluding, I seek to draw together in some ways, even as I also distinguish, the peace portraits and perspectives presented for each classroom; in reflecting further thus, I also seek to entertain the meanings and makings of our dreams of and dreaming for peace, and potential pedagogies for such, that are made possible by listening to and learning from children themselves.

Designing Dialogue with Children around Depictions of Peace and Violence

Recruited, most gratefully, to this particular work by and through the initiative of a distinguished colleague and former doctoral student, Dr. Debbie Sonu, my involvement in the elementary classrooms of former students, now teachers engaged in pedagogical endeavors related to the pursuit of peace, and with children therein, was undertaken with Dr. Sonu, and as part of a larger study involving additional grade schools, teachers, and children in New York City. At the time, I was simply investigating my own graduate students'—prospective teachers'—images and ideas of peace, and subsequent thoughts on teaching for peace, as reflected upon via photographs taken in the course of living. Dr. Sonu, however, concerned with her own education students' fears and reservations about engaging elementary children in important social issues in social studies—necessarily pertaining to issues of violence and peace—procured a grant through her university; sought not only to find elementary teachers in New York City embarking upon this work, but also to hear from children themselves in such settings regarding their understandings of peace and violence and the role their teachers, classrooms, and schools play and might play in teaching about such concerns. Three of my former students, as teachers in two elementary classrooms working with students around questions of violence and/or peace, became a part of this larger study, along with the children in their classrooms.[1]

Drawing upon my own experiences with these teachers, and observations and interviews commenced during this study, in Chapter 5 I sought to present portraits of their two school communities and classrooms and curricula, and focus on the teachers themselves: their conceptions of peace (and violence), and teaching commitments pertaining to the work of peace (and problem of violence). Here, I hope to build from and on such portraits, in setting forth something of the images, ideas, and understandings of children respecting such, as issuing from our directed work with some of them in each classroom over the course of a few months: conversing with them about peace and violence, and the roles their teachers, schools, and communities play in addressing violence and promoting peace. In each classroom, the teachers selected four to six children with whom we were able to hear from in this way, via individual interviews and focus-group activities and discussions on six or more separate occasions in May and June of 2011. Such choices were made largely based on student interest and parental consent, as well as sensitivity to diverse representation (that is, considerations of gender, ethnicity, background, perspective) and capacity for participation (that is, willingness to speak and engage). Our interviews with these teachers also illuminated further additional reasons for the selection of each

---

1To learn more about this larger study, and findings and publications issuing from it, see the work of Dr. Debbie Sonu, Hunter College, City University of New York.

particular child, to which I will return later in my introductions and presentations of the children's views on and visions of peace.[2]

In seeking to elucidate how children subjectively construct notions of peace and violence, such conceptions were explored with elementary students in a number of ways. First, we talked with children about peace and its opposite by asking each to draw a peaceful world and speak from their artworks about what makes for peace and what gets in the way of realizing it. Then, we read to students the classic folktale *Hansel and Gretel*[3] —one we felt possessed material generative for discussion around issues of peace and violence—and discussed the students' responses to the characters and their actions. In subsequent sessions, we engaged students in developing their own fictional characters—one representing peace and another, its nemesis—and stories involving these characters. For each of these collective activities, six to seven sessions in full, we worked with the children for about 45 minutes. We concluded the study with individual interviews of about 20 minutes each, reflectively clarifying comments made by students previously, and understandings articulated.

Providing students with disposable cameras to capture moments of peace or of its absence in their own lives in and out of school contexts, we also sought to make and draw connections between

---

2 I want to particularly thank and honor Callie Heilmann, a graduate student of Dr. Sonu, who tirelessly transcribed all recorded interviews and focus-group meetings, and for all her invaluable contributions to this work and study.

3 The story of Hansel and Gretel is one of hunger, poverty, and betrayal; sadness and suffering; violence and victory; and, of course, peaceful resolutions as suggested in a "happily-ever-after" ending. The tale tells of a stepmother who convinces the father to leave his children deep in the forest, as they are poor and do not have enough food for all of them. In the forest the children are drawn to a house made of candy, albeit owned by a witch who eats children. She enslaves the two of them, and has Gretel work while she works to fatten up Hansel in a cage to be later cooked and served as her meal. The old women, then planning to cook Gretel first, tries to trick her into the oven by asking her to check its readiness. Yet, she is outsmarted by Gretel, who pushes the witch in the oven and releases Hansel. The two children are delighted to gather all the witch's treasures for themselves and their father, who happily finds and reunites with them, also in the aftermath of their stepmother's death. For a full reading, see Lesser (1984), the beautifully illustrated version we used with the children in this study.

children's personal situations and circumstances and their unique and singular expressions of peace and violence. Herein, through individual interviews, animated by students' reflections upon their own photographs, we also created a different kind of space for children to talk about peace and violence, issuing from their own lives and framed by their own ideas, rather than in responsive dialogue and engagement with peers and other texts and directives, as in focus groups. Culminating this work, in this way, for me, offered a kind of synthesizing attention to student understandings of peace and violence, and also honored the import of subjectivity and experience in any passions for and pursuits of peace in the world. Given my parallel work with prospective teachers around picturing peace via photography as well, what follows in my presentations of the peace profiles gleaned from these children—while building from all the work undertaken with them—focuses largely upon study of their photographs and thoughts about them as expressed in these final interviews.

I got excited about peace because…I am really good at peace, I am a peacemaker![4]

My time in the first-grade classroom of Ruth and Derrick at Believe Charter School in East Harlem was spent largely with a highly animated and enthusiastic group of children, four[5] particularly, with whom I had the opportunity to engage in talking about their ideas and experiences of peace through the culminating photography project at the conclusion of our study—three boys and one girl. Two of the boys were African American; the third boy, seemingly bi-racial, perhaps of Afro-Hispanic origins; and the girl, Latina. All identified themselves as peacemakers, and that most avidly too.

---

4 This heading comes directly from one of the first-grade participants in this study, Bill, in an interview on 6/21/11.

5 While we had the privilege of working with some six to seven students through the course of this study at Believe Charter School, unfortunately largely due to frequent absences, with only four of them did we have sustained engagement through to the completion of the project.

Bill, tall and thin with shining eyes and brown skin, was affectionately called "President Bill" and "Mr. Peace" by his teachers—highly articulate, academically advanced, and something of a class leader. Such were some of the reasons his teachers thought of him for this study, described by Ruth (6/21/11) also as "complicated and amazing," and "deep and reflective." Another important quality mentioned concerned Bill's high standards for himself and disappointment when he does not meet them. In my first encounter with this young African American boy, I was immediately struck by the seriousness, focus, and maturity he brought to our work together, as well as the eagerness, joy, and charisma.

Smaller and more solid of frame than Bill, Reggie was often moving and laughing, and also had a lot to say and share. What comes to mind for me in thinking now about him is his beautiful black face, beaming with an infectious smile, and big bright eyes. Derrick (6/21/11), in speaking of him, highlighted his interest in his karate class and close-knit group of friends, whose parents were also close. Ruth (6/21/11) spoke of him as a "preacher" who "knows all the prayers"—a kid who is "full of wonder," "curious," "passionate and funny." In my experience with Reggie, I found him also to be highly engaged in our inquiries together, and deeply sensitive—even upset by certain demonstrations he recognized as at odds with peace, and as obstacles to freedom.

Lean and lively, Parnes is an adorable character to whom one is readily drawn. Quick to move and speak, he makes himself known. With his smooth coffee-colored skin, sparkling big brown eyes, long eyelashes, and long dark wavy ponytail, he has a striking presence in the classroom. Ruth (6/21/11) says of him:

> He is incredibly unique…and creative and…does a really good job of being himself. He also really…struggles with focus and following expectations because he is so original…is way ahead of everybody in most subjects.

He was selected because of these traits, also because he "thrives on attention" and has been helped by the peace corner "in the moments when he is about to have a tantrum."

Grace, a petite Latina girl, greeted me upon each visit with a sweet smile and hug. She often wore her dark, shiny straight hair in side ponytails. Her warmth was matched by a shy, quiet, and soft-spoken disposition. A twin whose sister is in another class, she reportedly is very close to her sister, and actually quite social with a core group of good friends. Because Grace was so slow to speak, though, in our work together, I found it surprising that she was chosen and volunteered for this study. Her teachers did express a desire to bring her out, and afford her opportunities for participation, as well as acknowledge a certain uniqueness of perspective she possessed, describing her not only as "cute" but also "fiery" (Ruth, 6/21/11).

"I took a picture of myself," Reggie (6/21/11) proudly announces, "because I am a peacemaking man." In looking at the photographs these first-graders at the Believe Charter School took to document peace in their own lives, and interviewing them at the close of our site-based study, a dominant perspective on peace stands out: the classic idea that "peace begins with me." Self-portraits were among the highest number of photographs taken by each child—himself or herself, smiling, mostly standing, inside or outside: in front of a classroom window, tree, playground, garden of flowers, or piece of artwork at school or home. Some also had the child playfully reaching his or her arms out, as if to hug another; and others, displays of pride in showcasing a piece of school work—a drawing created, story written, math assignment well done. In related conversation, these children spoke about peace largely in relation to their own actions: for example, meditating, calming down and relaxing; discovering and finding out new things; "using your words" and stopping fights; being kind to, caring for, and sharing with others; and not throwing trash on the floor, but rather making the earth healthy. This emphasis, too, reflects one they encounter consistently via the curriculum, teaching, and classroom management and community practice enacted by their teachers.

People—particularly family members, friends, peers, and teach-ers—were among the next ranking peace focus depicted in the photos of these first-graders. The child was present, as well, in many of these shots, reflecting the importance of relationships with others, and especially significant others, and loved ones. In fact, all of these youngsters, at some point in the interviews, identified some person or more as representing peace and even inspiring peace in him or her, or to pursue peace. Parnes' sister embodies peace to him:

> because my sister is there…, because my sister likes to play with me a lot. She gives me a hug and a high-five and sometimes she says "I love you."…. Because I love her so much with all my heart and she loves me with all her heart. (6/21/11)

He also mentions another teacher in the pull-out program who takes him to a special room during the class day and gives him special toys to play with and activities in which to engage. Other children mention others in their lives—mom, dad, twin sister, friend, teacher (Ruth and Derrick), and even Martin Luther King, Jr. These individuals were most described, as well, as good, helpful, caring, nonviolent and "for peace." A focus, too, was placed on their use of words, presumably in contrast to acts of aggression or violence.

Smiles also abounded in these photographs featuring people—what looked like laughing too, and hugging; and in many of these images, people were engaged in some kind of activity as well: swinging on swings or sliding down slides at a playground, reading together on a classroom carpet or home couch, one person assisting another with school work or demonstrating how to use a camera, and showcasing together something created like a painting, story, or "peace character." Scenes depicted herein included background sights, such as the subway, a birthday cake, a shared meal, an Obama "Yes We Can" poster, a New York City health fair advocacy sign, and a rooftop garden. Additional photos led me to believe that such places and accouterments were not insignificant.

Indeed, students' photographs incorporated in this way, as well as singularly depicted and honed in on, peace as related to such particular events or activities, places, or settings, and objects or ideas. For example, Reggie featured his father's birthday party, as he explained the love of his dad and the expression of such, and also because it was a joyous occasion with delicious cake and ice cream. Separately, Grace described peace in this manner: "It looks like, like, you are going to be invited to a party" (6/16/11). For Parnes, similarly, a family outing to Sizzler's for a nourishing and festive dinner was featured. Home, school, art, and nature figured prominently here as well, and as reflecting some kind of health and harmony therein. Foregrounded in many photos, or even just in their backgrounds, were parks, gardens, skies, trees, flowers, vines, or windows christened with sunlight. Artwork, though most featured was the children's own, also often depicted the natural world, such as a mural at their school of verdant foliage along with butterflies, birds, bobcats, and other animals. Such artifacts, along with other classwork displayed, also reflected a sense of peace that is allied with accomplishment, pride in one's own creative expressions or intellectual powers.

School was thus also considered to be a peaceful place—"mostly"[6]—as well as a place where peace was taught. Most of the children referenced in conversation, or took pictures of, some aspect of the peace curriculum in their classroom, such as the peace corner, peace signs, peace puppets, or their own artwork of peace characters.

Knowledge was often affiliated with peace here as well, and/or ignorance with its absence. As a source of learning, Bill explicitly identifies school with peace. A lover of math and science, he says, "science is peace because they find out new things and they discover it" (6/21/11); he also speaks about realizing peace with respect to learning peace, in *knowing* that you can change, that you can be and do peace. Grace shares that she didn't know peace until she was shown peace by her teachers; and alternately in one example of peace's opposite, she had a photo of litter on the ground, of which she said, "people throwing trash because they don't know nothing" (6/21/11).

All of the children, however, spoke most highly of home as a place of peace—and represented such in their photos, particularly in relation to being cared for and loved, and to sharing together. While not so much in the photographs or conversation issuing from them, the figure of the mother was central to many in some of our previous focus-group discussions, such that here the import of the home, too, may be allied in some way with the maternal, and feminine, regarding peace. The import of agency and freedom to the experience of peace may have figured within such portraits as well—as also perhaps depicted in images from children of playgrounds and playing

---

6 Instances of fighting, bullying, chaos, and noise were cited as occurring in schools, and at odds with peace.

fields for baseball and other games in which recreation, openness, and choice are central. Parnes reports that when he needs and chooses to meditate, for example, peace is "wherever I go" (6/21/11). "Peace is like if you want to move," Reggie proclaims, or "just relax in nature, it's peaceful and there is nothing around you that can boss you around" (6/21/11).

These young "peacemakers" are also largely focused on peace, rather than its absence. Very few of their photos depict scenes or "somethings" in want of or calling for peace, and Reggie, for instance, even refuses to make a character who represents the opposite of peace in one of our focus-group activities, creating two peace heroes instead.

In conversation, though, these children thoughtfully highlight a number of ideas concerning what is counter to peace, and/or hinders its realization. Here, they speak of things like anger, apathy, agitation, oppression, ugliness, suffering, destructiveness, violence, and revenge. Grace identifies particular acts affiliated with such things like littering, screaming, fighting, and "destroying a party." Bill focuses on bullying and violence that may come from being mad, sad, bored, or selfish and/or alienated from others. He postulates:

> "...Bad people shoot and then they die...maybe because...they want their way.... Maybe they think they're really sad and tired of it and they don't care if their friends want them to [stop bullying or doing violence]..." (6/21/11)

He also mentions the influence of parents who encourage their children to acts of aggression. Parnes (6/21/11), relatedly, notes that while violence—defined mostly here in relation to hitting—is "bad," he feels compelled to it: "...sometimes I do violence in school because they hit me. My dad told me, 'If someone hits you, you got to hit them back.'" Herein, too, are allusions to differences in school and home expectations and practices, often difficult for children to negotiate and navigate.

Parnes, too, articulates in some ways a markedly different perspective on peace via its opposite or absence than the other children. Here, he lucidly speaks about the powerful relationship between desire and violence—which he associates with hurt feelings and wanting to "get back" at others who have hurt you, in addition to teasing, bragging, hitting, bullying, and killing. Noting the cyclical nature of this relationship too, he concludes: "Most people don't want peace because they like being mean to each other.... they like fighting" (6/21/11). While distinguishing between real and play guns and wars, he affirms, too, his own pleasure in video games his dad once tried to keep him from because they were "too violent"—and their seductive allure. "I like the way, how they play because they have, like, cool guns. They put colors on them," he explains. Reggie (6/21/11), in contrast, in speaking of contexts of violence, finds a way to make peace the more desirable option: "One person's got to be the heroine." His emphasis respecting obstacles to peace include feelings of jealousy and sadness; and conditions in which one is hit, pushed, lied to, and/or bossed around; additionally, he speaks at length about the experiences of poverty, homelessness, and hunger.

> ...people want to make peace, but the other people don't because they don't know about peace. (Parnes, 6/21/11)

Parnes demonstrates the complexities, and even contradictions, involved in these children's understandings, experiences, and ideas of peace, and its opposite. While in one instance, he claims that people don't really want peace, in another, he suggests that they do, and— with the other children—that a lack of knowledge prevents people from embracing peace in their lives. In this sense, though, all of the children express a firm belief that peace can and should be taught— peace as something you can come to know and do and live. In the negative, Parnes focuses on teaching people not to ignore others, and particularly, not to throw trash on the floor. Both points emphasize an ethics of respect. Parnes suggests positive practices for promoting peace, including listening and using your words, making the peace sign and giving "high fives," hugging and saying "I love you," "giving peace" to animals and making the earth healthy, and playing "with toys and stuff" and "reading better." Such ideas, interestingly, reflect attention to both the language and practice of ethics, and of desire.

All of the children herein focus on teaching peace as related to "giving peace" and on the use of words in such giving, rather than acts of violence in expressing oneself and in relating to others. For Grace, this actively involves teaching others to stop fights, and a turn to authorities like teachers and policemen for help with such. Reggie spoke of teaching each child to be the hero in such interventions, and with Bill, to offer peaceful alternatives in situations of conflict. Reggie also highlights the pedagogical use of peace puppets in role-playing and practicing to resolve arguments. Here, the curricular use of peace puppets and peace patrols in their classroom seem to have been implicitly if not explicitly referenced by the children. Bill (6/21/11) was the most direct and specific in his ideas for teaching peace, ideas also reflective of a belief in the power of words and dialogue for promoting peace and change:

> If I was a teacher I would first, I would send out signs of, like, peace in the world to adults first, then I would go to little kids and teach them about peace.... I would go in different classes.... It would be, let us get in a circle and every Thursday and Monday we are going to talk about peace and how we can do it.... by like telling them that peace is kindness in the world and ... I would tell them no more violence because it's going to be bad for you. You are going to blow up with violence instead of using your words... and "You can change," and say peace things—"You know you can do it," like that.

Additionally, this teaching peace as "giving peace" envisioned and voiced by these students was indelibly tied to love and generosity: Bill spoke of it in relation to kindness and conversation; Parnes, to listening and loving; and Reggie, to helping and heroism. As Grace (6/21/11) put it, we must teach, "caring for each other at all times."

"My inquiry class...working on what might cause violence... Ways we might stop [it]"[7]

Five highly engaged, often quite serious, fourth-graders—two girls and three boys—from Dorothy's class at P.S. 1722 in the South Bronx were recruited to and voluntarily participated in this peace/violence

---

7 This heading comes from the words of Marnie, a participant in this study with fourth-graders, in an interview conducted on 6/14/11.

study with my colleague and me, and undertook the photography exercise to conclude it. Many are of Dominican or Mexican heritage, all but one are biracial children of color; all live in the neighborhood, have in some way experienced or witnessed violence therein, and are concerned about the question of violence there and in general.

"We don't have much time," Marnie says to me, her green eyes sparkling, as she pulls her sandy-brown hair back and up into a ponytail. "So I am going to talk about these pictures" (6/24/11). The bright, clear, light-brown skin of this biracial young woman shines all the more, it seems, as she gives me her gentle smile. Her direct, yet soft-spoken manner, while warm and engaging, appears ever to be somewhat serious, focused on the task at hand—and this in contrast often to her peers. Shorter and fuller of frame than many of the girls in her class, Marnie has a kind of maternal appeal and presence, firm and also nurturing in her relationships with others. Recently, she had informed her teacher in written form that she might appear sad for a while as she just learned of her parents' upcoming divorce. In this way, her teacher (Dorothy, 6/24/11) describes her as "like an adult already," "like a CEO," and "really with-it"—affording a unique contribution to our study, and certain to be engaged and conversant. Relatedly, she reportedly has "no patience for silliness," a positive influence on others in relation to such directed study, as well.

A rather striking young woman, taller and more developed than most other girls her age, Johanna enters the room with a sense of gentleness and grace, her long, dark, wavy hair framing her face, and her big, soft-brown eyes and warm, wide smile. Thoughtful with keen insight, she seems to find herself at a challenging stage wherein she wants to be popular with the boys, yet finds herself somewhat afraid of them; and relatedly, facing conflicting desires and decisions about her directions ahead academically and socially. This context for Johanna as described by her teacher, and part of her rationale for inviting Johanna to this study, was confirmed in my many interactions with her, and I was delighted to spend time with such a bright and articulate young woman, dialoguing together with refreshing frankness and honesty about issues of peace and violence as pertaining to such a critical juncture in her own life and growth.

I met Jason—a small, lithe young man with a playfully disheveled head of light brown hair, and one of the few White children in this class—on my first visit to the school. An outgoing conversationalist, he approached and welcomed me, a boyish grin on his face and smiling green eyes, and shared with me a "corny" joke. Talkative and humorous, Jason is described by his teacher, Dorothy (6/24/11), as also a bit mischievous: he enjoys pitting co-teachers against each other and has a flare for the dramatic. She thought of him for this study, she says, because he "sees things a little differently than other people might.... He always knows what is going on. He never pays attention to what he should be."

A gentle and good-natured young man of Hispanic descent with short dark hair and a stocky frame, Jim strides into the room with a smile and a greeting. When he speaks, I'm struck by the originality and thoughtfulness of his ideas. His teacher, Dorothy, says of him: "Jim has a big voice... a way of being able to see things from other perspectives and question." She speaks, too, of "his amazing creativity." His knowledge of world affairs and his sensitivity also recommended him to her for this study. His giftedness as an artist and subtle humor enhanced our work together for me as well.

Small but fiery, John is a light-skinned African American fourth-grader, who has a strong presence in the classroom among his teachers and peers. Tending to do and say whatever he wants whenever he wants, he has been described by other students as a bully and by teachers as a troublemaker, or troubled. Articulate, forceful, and at times highly serious, I found his capacity for conversation to be strong, and for disrupting such, though, equally as strong. In this, despite his academic and behavioral challenges, John demonstrates keen intelligence and leadership potential. With his hair short and tightly framing his face, small penetrating brown eyes and thin wiry frame, when he smiles, it lights up his whole face and lightens his countenance, and his humor ignites raucous response, especially from his male peers. His teachers, given his classroom identity and interest, readily advanced his participation, and also because such might afford the opportunity for some kind of success for him in school.

"When I need somebody, they [sic] always there" (Johanna, 6/24/11); Johanna explains why the many photographs she has taken of her friends represent peace to her. Indeed, photographs of people—friends, family members, and teachers—tend to rank first in number for these fourth-graders in their portrayals of peace in their own lives. Additionally, what is highlighted herein are largely the relationships the student has with the person and people being depicted—ones of love, trust, belonging, security, growth, goodness, joy, care, and recognition. "Peace is, to me, like my mom and dad," John (6/24/11) says, and of a photo of his mom and him hugging and smiling together for the camera on a park bench, he adds: "I'm safe with Mom and she with me." Jason (6/24/11) similarly explains: "Parents tell you how to do good things so you won't do bad things." Many also took photographs of their teachers and spoke of them in relation to peace in terms of the very act of teaching kids, and of trying to make a difference in their lives and in the world.

Still, by far the greatest number of photos in this area, and discussion, were oriented around the presence of friends in the lives of these young people, both inside and outside of school. This finding, contrasting somewhat with what was was illuminated through this work by first-graders, tends to confirm developmental research suggesting that youth in pre-teen and teen years are more strongly interested in and influenced during this period of their lives by their peers than by family members or teachers, at least subjectively so in their own minds. Johanna specifically spoke about one shot she took of her friend who helped her with the bake sale initiated to raise money to send relief in the aftermath of the earthquake in Japan. Warmth, friendliness, and kindness were oft-mentioned characteristics describing such friends who brought peace into these youth's lives.

In a rather sweet way they also included here a number of pictures of each other—for example, Johanna of Marnie, Marnie of Johanna, and John of Jim—as friends and sources of peace for one another, in addition to numerous friends who were not a part of this study. Jim (6/24/11) had taken a picture of Johanna smiling, of which he said: "because she is my friend, and she seems peaceful...very nice, and she likes people being nice back to her." Jason (6/24/11), too, included photos of Johanna and spoke not only of such things but also of how "fun and funny" Johanna is—peace and pleasure, and reciprocity, allied. Another interesting aspect herein noted, which alas

I did not follow up on, was that Jason took a picture of Johanna's form, possibly honing in on her breasts, at a time in which her bra was showing a bit, accentuating further perhaps the relationship between peace and desire or passion, perhaps here his emerging sexuality. During my time in this classroom, I had considered the possibility that Jason might have a bit of a crush on Johanna—and there had been some commentary from his teachers concerning this as well—because he typically engaged her more than others, and often playfully teased her.

Common threads relating to the context and content embraced in such photos included friends—and to a lesser extent family members and teachers—hugging, smiling, holding hands, walking, talking, laughing, taking pictures, and eating. Many featured, as well, playgrounds and park-like settings, including sky and water; symbols of peace, such as the American flag, the Statue of Liberty, or a t-shirt worn displaying the peace sign (one read: "Only Natural Highs" on it), or person giving the peace sign or making a muscle; and in the classroom, showcasing students working well together or some award board for student-honored work. Herein, too, the import of memory in relation to peace seems to be implicitly affirmed as much offered here represented a hearkening back to good times or humorous moments, and past achievements and joys. A shared school field trip to the Statue of Liberty was featured in some way by all of these children, of which Jason (6/24/11) noted: "It was wonderful there, and we saw lots of things."

Some interesting absences of note—especially in contrast to that of the first-graders with whom I worked—are that while some of the students included themselves in a few photos with friends, by in large, they did not feature themselves in their depictions of peace, and took no such singular photos of themselves in identifying as peaceful or a peacemaker. Additionally, only Jim took a photo, and but one, of a woman in solitude and quiet reverie, in exploring the idea and experience of peace. In it, she was on the ferry, sitting alone, contemplatively looking out at the water and horizon before her. He spoke, likewise, of retreat, even detachment, at times as a way to achieve peace or as a peace practice.

It is difficult to know exactly what to make of this, if in relation to a time period where peer relationships are so central in the minds and lives of students—the self being discerned largely via the gaze of others, or not, or signifying something else altogether. The pedagogy in the classroom, as focused on critical inquiry into violence, and action in response to such, largely collective, also did not directly take up notions of or practices of peace in relation to one's individual identity as peacemaker or practice in relation to solitude, withdrawal, or contemplation, which many associate with a kind of non-action. These absences, then, may reflect the context in which the study was undertaken; even perhaps the dominance of friends, classmates, and school-related engagements in the photos as well, as this group of five fourth-graders worked together throughout our study in a most sustained and concerted way, more so than the first-graders, such that the photography project itself may have been undertaken through the lens of school predominantly, subjective lived experience beyond such perhaps somewhat obscured therein.

Additionally, as possibly a function of age and experience, these students underscored in their work and dialogue the complexity of peace as embodied or not within people—friend, family member, self, or other. John, in fact, did not even depict people as his top representation of peace, and many more people he featured were actually from newspaper accounts of violence, but herein he was the exception, to which I will return in later discussion. Most, though, depicted some individuals in their lives—in addition to those who brought them peace—as representatives almost exclusively at odds with peace. All of these children spoke of some people as both peaceful and "unpeaceful"—lacking peace, or in some cases even the opposite of peace, depending upon mood, moment, context, or interaction. Johanna (6/24/11) depicted certain friends and her brother in this light. She emphasized the problems of being annoyed or "bugged" by such people in her life. Jim (6/24/11) spoke at length about a girl he does not like who will not leave him alone, even when he demands it, but rather "tries to make me talk to her" and "pinches my cheeks hard and it hurts." Marnie (6/24/11) spoke of her cousin generally in relation to peace's opposite, in his affinity for "picking fights" and his "negative talk." Jim, Jason, and Marnie each qualified their images of one of their teachers as a man of peace, except when mean or mad, which were discussed in terms of students "getting on his nerves," "speaking over," or "not listening" to him, not putting things away, or "doing the wrong thing."

It is worth mentioning, concerning people in relation to peace, as well as violence, the heightened and complex role that gender seemed to play in student portrayals and considerations. While gendered conceptions emerged in such discussions with first-graders, they were largely unaddressed in their photographs and talk about them, although an affiliation of home with peace might be taken up in its relation to the feminine, and the figure of the mother was emphasized by the youngsters at other times in conversation. Here, however, with these fourth-graders, home was not only spoken about more ambiguously as a place of peace, or not, at times; but also neither mother nor father, nor parents or relatives broadly, were figures of emphasis or focus: only John (6/24/11), for example, explicitly took a photograph of his mother, and emphasized her as the strongest source of peace in his life and inspiration to peace. He tells a tragic story of his aunt who was shot outside the laundromat, caught in gun crossfire, and his mom there with her who survived, adding: "and now my mom hates guns." The peace character he created during one of our focus-group activities together was also female, a counselor who helped troubled youth, while the character opposed to peace was male—abused girls, was in a gang, and killed for sport.[8] When I inquired with him about these choices, he said for peace he "decided the woman because women are mostly getting hurt a lot... and then so I put a woman that was trying to stop it. She's a strong woman..."

The majority of John's photos, in fact, were not only those depicting violence in some way, or the opposite of or call for peace, but many of these also featured gun and gang violence by males, and violence against women. Gendered considerations accompany these

---

8 Interestingly, John was the only student who did not create characters of the same gender in his embodied explorations of peace and its opposite. Identified as a bully by others, and in many ways self-identifying this way as well, his violent character was male. The other students created figures of the same gender, and allied with the gender to which each identified (that is, the girls created female figures, the other boys created male figures).

photos in his discussion of them, as well, though in such he also reveals his complex and conflicted views:

> ...males are killing the girls, so they are the victims....
> Girls get more.... She probably did something by mistake....
> I think he was going to do something to those ladies.... I think he was abus-
> ing her... I see it in the world sometimes when peoples slap their girl-
> friends...because girls sometimes make you mad...they learned it from
> growing up, I think they learned it from their dad...

Of joining gangs, too, he concludes: "They're not manly enough to fight their own battles."

While Jim does not speak in this manner concerning such things, nor much about gender, he does identify a girl most strongly as his image of the opposite of peace: the one he does not like, who pinches his cheeks; she is the big bully in his life. Jason (6/24/11), similar to John, speaks of violence or peace's opposite more broadly, and most in relation to males—for him, involving gangs, guns, and drugs, and also "hookers" and abuse of women; yet, he also speaks at some length about women who drink and shouldn't have children, and "just leave their kids [at daycare] 'cause they want to leave them, and...they be selling drugs."

Meanwhile, Johanna actually identifies John himself quite une-quivocally with the opposite of peace, and actively with violence. This fact alone created a very particular context throughout the study in which Johanna generally wished to work with us alone, or part-nered with Marnie, and was expressly hesitant to voice her opinions where John was present or if she feared he would get word of what she had to say. She speaks here too of the male students, reporting that they "bring bad stuff in, always a fight in class...boys more violent than girls. Usually all the fights we have in this class or outside because boys starting the fights" (Johanna, 6/24/11). Interest-ingly, though, neither of the girls in this study specifically identified girls as stronger forces for peace than boys, nor even mentioned sexual violence, whereas the boys did both, in many ways. Two important factors concerning gender herein, too, may surely have issued from their backgrounds—religious, cultural, and perhaps class—reflecting the influence of rather strong and somewhat tradi-tional gender roles in their lives. Their teacher, Dorothy, mentioned more than once her students' abiding concern expressed over the fact that she was not married nor had any children, and was well into her 20s. Additionally, amid profound hormonal and physical body changes, attention to and awareness of sexuality and gender differentiation tend to be heightened in preteens at this time, developmentally.

However, what emerges, then, is a much stronger focus on peace's opposite, or violence, or perhaps obstacles to peace, rather than peace itself, in the positive, in a number of ways (and definitely more strongly than seen with the first-graders in this study). This could be perceived as aligning with the ways in which peace is generally formally defined, such as in dictionaries, for instance. Herein, explicating peace is undertaken largely in terms of *absence*— for example, of turmoil, suffering, discord, conflict, war, oppression, or violence. Additionally, this emphasis of these students may issue from and be more clearly resonant with the focus of their classroom inquiry study on the question of violence in their lives and communities. Of the study, Johanna (6/14/11) reports: "We came up with...that because we always be talking about what's going on in the streets, happening to us...in my neighborhood, it looks like drugs, shooting out...." Sadly, in this way too, a greater focus on violence, the opposite of peace, or the absence of peace, may reflect something more central to their life situations than the positive experience of peace.

Obstacles to peace and instigations to violence arise here, too, for these students not only in terms of gender, but also of race and of class. Marnie (6/14/11) explains: "Mostly you could see how people.... like about race...going into a store, and 'ooh, get out of here, you are Black.' A Black person might not like it and fight back. They just don't like them, but that still don't give them the right to say that." Most of the children identify Martin Luther King, Jr., as well, as one of the most emblematic and inspiring representatives of peace of whom they have ever known, and in his fighting the violence of racism and racial injustice. Of famous embodiments of the opposite of peace, also included by most, was the figure of King's assassin. This shared finding may or may not have something to do with the curriculum in school, and/or a shared identity as children of color. Jason

(6/14/11), too, a White boy, is inspired by King, in that "he was fighting for other peoples, so they could all be in school." He continues: "...most of my friends are colored...we couldn't talk..."

Comments are made about being jobless and homeless in relation to peace's absence or its hindrance, as well, by students—some, only in their depictions of characters antithetical to peace, but others, in discussing their photographs as well; in fact, John took a photo of a man sleeping on a park bench, whom he describes as poor, alone, and without home or money. Interestingly, however, socioeconomic antagonisms at odds with peace also involve wealth acquired, its use, and attitudes pertaining to it—Jason (6/24/11) describes this scene:

> ...'Cuz now people just don't care...they don't have feelings for anyone.... They just think about themselves. Like if they are rich, "hood rich".... When you are hood rich, you want so much, you turn everybody else to the side...

Marnie (6/24/11) shares similarly, separately, how "sometimes it could be 'hood rats' [or 'hood rich,' recording unclear].... Sometimes people like that, they like nice things; violence happens trying to take things from other people."

Images students showcase to depict the opposite of peace also include their classroom that was "trashed" by workers who came in to actually repair something, trash cans overflowing and with garbage on the floor, dirty floors and descending stairs, walls with peeling paint, graffiti and written curse words, staged portrayals of boys fighting, men with baggy pants that show their underwear, and newspaper clippings or signs featuring various forms of violence or tragedy. Marnie focuses on an accident she had, which left her incapacitated for a long time, as well as depressed, and the nightmares she still has about the event sometimes. Herein, again, is highlighted the import of memory, memories that can hurt and haunt the individual. She also talks, though, about cyber-bullying, and how thoughtlessness, indifference, or a lack of care can work against peace. Jim (6/24/11), too, highlights a time he fell and was hurt when an area at school was left uncared for and unattended—floors dirty, slippery, unkempt—and those who don't care, "not with us anymore...because they just don't want to...deal..."

Johanna (6/24/11), meanwhile, elucidates these potential forces at odds with peace:

> Sometimes they might write in bad words and stuff, they are damaging property...outside of school... 'cuz they think it is fun, don't think they are damaging nothing.... Because they mad, want to start problems....
> ....She thought if she doesn't do bad, they won't pay attention to her.
> ...because they probably in the days people did something bad to them, so they want to do it back to other people.

We find attention given here to the problems of ignorance, anger, revenge, and a lack of recognition, among other things—including a sense of the cyclical nature by which violence begets violence. In this regard, Marnie (6/14/11) comments: "I don't think anyone is born that way [violent or opposed to peace].... experiencing it, living around it, in their surroundings...if their parents are always fighting, in the streets, if they see knives..." Still, in moments, there is also a hearkening to desire in relation to that which opposes peace—the "fun" or pleasure of destroying property for instance, and perhaps related to a sense or feeling of visibility or empowerment.

John (6/14/11) alludes to such in locating the cause of violence in "the gangs and the guns," as he also reports that he really likes guns. "Peace goes on in my block a little," he continues, "but violence takes control of peace.... In my neighborhood, some people don't feel safe. It's sad because peoples can't have a good time. It's like the gangs take over our freedom.... Every day you see somebody taking advantage of our freedom.... Cops don't have no [sic] control of the gangs." Of the shootings in his community, Jason (6/14/11) says: "It's sort of like action... no, it's not fun, but people want to know what is happening. It's fun when cool stuff happens, but sometimes inappropriate." This idea launches him into a discussion also of so-called violent and/or sexually explicit video games, toying with the idea that you can have a "little bit" of peace and violence, but not "too much," or "take it too far." Indirectly, Jason (6/24/11), as well, associates a lack of peace with a lack of freedom, albeit via the internal condition of addiction, or simply drunkenness: "I pass by the liquor store a lot and I always see drunk people.... They are seeking peace, maybe, but aren't peaceful." At least, herein though, the desire for peace is felt to be present and operative.

These youth do return to peace, happily then, in their photographic explorations, from this preponderance of antithetical images and conversations around them—particularly in presenting key symbols of peace, in order to call this hope to mind, to inspire and intend and pursue it. Such peace representations are embraced, as well, in images of nature, art, and religion, in addition to symbols of peace as symbols—like the peace sign, V-hand gesture, or the word "peace" painted on a wall, in English or another language; though even the former are often spoken of as symbols for peace as well (e.g., like a sculpture of an angel or painting of a dove). The plethora of peace portraits depicted emblematically did have me wondering, though, if such suggested peace as more fully an ideal in the minds of these students, a dream in hopes of realizing, than something grounded in their lived experiences to which they could concretely point, and that they could clearly and easily photograph. Developmentally, too, these students may be engaging the world more abstractly than, say, the first-graders are, such that they are especially drawn to exploring symbols; yet, for me, the critique of many scholars who posit and articulate the ways in which ours is a culture of violence, and into which we educate our children, began resonating more loudly in my ears as I noted this trend with these fourth-graders. I asked myself if it were possible that these students have been unlearning peace, and/or learning violence via their schooling, and in the course of their formal education.

Issuing from a class field trip to Liberty Island, no doubt, all of the students took manifold photos featuring Lady Liberty as a sign of peace, as well as street entertainers in costume as such, and wrapped in the American flag. Marnie (6/24/11) explains this choice:

> Statue of Liberty—she's, like, she brings peace to everyone, she represents all our liberties... no one can make you do something, like you can't be in trouble unless you can prove you did it.

Other symbols captured through this outing included by many were also images of the American flag, and also of a policeman, and with his gun or focusing on his gun holder or badge, and a security officer. Talk around such depictions involved the ideals of freedom and liberty, as well as ideas of authority, power, security, protection, and keeping the peace. Here, John photographed, as well, the Liberty motorcycle; denoting, for him, not only freedom, agency, and power, but also because it was made for the purpose of giving back to one's country, in service, and because riding a motorcycle is also a pleasurable and exhilarating experience. Relatedly, he took pictures of the boat that took them to the island, emphasizing its speed in movement, impact on the water in the wake it made, its sound, and the feel of the wind on his face and body while riding it. Jim (6/24/11), perhaps relatedly, took a picture of a helicopter in the sky hovering over the water, peaceful because it "could get you places, give you news or weather reports..."

Most other depictions of the water that day, though, seemed to embrace a more reflective, quiet, and soothing aspect to peace as represented and discussed. From water to sky, from earth to heaven, students depicted such in many ways, indeed, as expressive of the peace nature affords, to which I will return, and yet also as something symbolically depicting peace. Of a photograph she took of the open sky with clouds, and then of another to follow that captured a piece of artwork in her home—an angel sculpture, Johanna (6/24/11) says:

> This picture is peaceful for me because, like, my uncle and my cousin died, so every time I look up, I know they always watching...and like the clouds sometimes do different things, make different shapes.
> Angels... they are peaceful because they remind me of my uncle and cousin.
> I got that one after my first communion so it reminds me of God and stuff...He is...good.

Johanna, though, is somewhat singular in an emphasis on religious icons, which include in other photos images of Mary and Jesus, and those featuring popular prayers. Marnie did, however, also feature a Christian cross on display in her house.

The other symbol students embraced in their work on peace was the peace symbol itself, and hand sign, and the printed word "peace," as made by friends, found on t-shirts, posted as signs, painted on walls, and presented in artwork. As their own school has the word "peace" in manifold different languages recursively painted throughout the stairwell, this signifier was a readily available one for all of them. Johanna, again, in describing her photos of a mural found in a nearby playground, speaks most, and most directly, about such:

> Peace signs on playground.... 'cuz they try to make a difference in the world.... Also 'cuz of the colors...butterflies, they remind me of peace...because they, like, something beautiful.

As students also depict art and nature for peace as in relation often to the experience of the beautiful, and not just symbolically, they include: flowers, trees, gardens, park greens, water and waves and rain, birds, and sky and light and clouds; as well as cityscapes and artworks depicting nature scenes and animals, like eagles, tigers, and puppies. Of such, Jason adds that we need water to live; Jim speaks of the beautiful natural background scenes in his photos that are peaceful; John emphasizes the sights and sounds of nature, and also talks about how funny birds are, how fun it is to watch them swim and dive and fly. Johanna similarly enjoys taking in the colors in nature and art, and the delightful smell of a fragrant flower. She includes the image of a "peaceful" safari scene too from art on a wall at home, depicting elephant mother and child joined by clasped trunks. In featuring nature, Marnie (6/24/11) offers insight into her process for photographing peace:

> I was at my aunt's house, and I went into the room and opened the window and took pictures of flowers, things like that.... When I was in my neighborhood ...I took a picture of the rain because I think the rain can be peaceful.

From this process, and reflecting upon it in sharing their thoughts about the photographs they had taken, these young people also had a bit to say to adults about how peace might be pursued or taught. Consistent with their appreciable attention to violence—or to that which prevents or hinders or thwarts the way of peace, all felt it important to teach children frankly about violence, its causes and sources, and how to respond in the face of it, as well as work to put an end to it. Marnie (6/14/11) tells me, "I think it's good that schools might teach children about violence because that person will never know if they are in danger...they might think something is funny and a good game but it's not." While she moves quickly to the site of the individual here, and matters of ignorance or misconception, John

(6/14/11) frames his discussion first, and more concretely, at the national level. "America is just wasted, like, wasted. You can't run anymore. They just take over the people because they have guns," he explains, and continues with his thoughts on possible solutions: "If I could speak to Obama, I would ask him if he could put the guns away, having cops going around people more often." Jason takes up larger social issues directly first, as well, relating to guns, drinking, drugs, and hookers; and ties them to individual behavior—or rather behaviors from which to abstain—and school policies and practices, recommending that schools be drug- and smoke-free zones, search students for weapons, and teach against related vices to which youth might be drawn. Johanna wishes even specifically for all-girl schools to make for more peaceful learning and relations.

Concerning education, schooling, and pedagogy, explicitly, John (6/24/11) emphasizes an agenda to "work to stop violence," that "school needs to talk about it, kids should know... and show them what they are supposed to do." While all students posit, here, a number of possibilities, what those might be are met with different and sometimes conflicting responses. For example, John recommends the practice of responding to a bully by bullying—"let them know what it feels like." Marnie (6/14/11) counters such with an appeal to understanding, conversation, and transformation: "I don't think anyone is born that way.... experiencing it, living around it, in their surroundings...if their parents are always fighting, in the streets, if they see knives..." She says that we need to "see why they think or do that," and work to "change their minds." Jim (6/24/11) similarly locates work against violence and for peace with self-knowledge, deemed acquired with age. Suggesting that older kids work with younger kids, he also affirms the importance of dialogue and inquiry: "First, talk about what is getting them angry, saying 'Sorry'..." With Jason, he emphasizes teaching withdrawal and detachment from moments of chaos or walking away from conflict, and this, in many ways, in relation to calming oneself down, and introducing a peaceful aspect to a charged environment.

The import of emotions, then too, and in learning to deal with them in ways that do not escalate anger but rather cultivate peace, is something all of these children address—in themselves and in their own lives, in the adults in their lives, as well as in terms of schools and teachers, and their efforts to teach for peace. Johanna speaks at length about wisely handling one's feelings, especially disappointment: learning to inquire and reflect before responding in situations, rather than just reacting. Jason (6/14/11) focuses a bit more on adults who "should not just get down—don't let your emotions fly out." Jim (6/24/11), speaking of the classroom context, advises:

> If I was a teacher, I wouldn't get mad, I would know it's not their fault that they [students] need to play a lot...talk to parents about what they do, sometimes, and help them learn ways to calm themselves down.... Some kids might be bored of school so they might want to goof off sometimes.

From such emerges a compelling pedagogical point, as well, affirmed in varied ways by all of the students—that educational work for peace, countering that which opposes peace, includes making space for play, choice, voice, interest, and inquiry in curriculum, teaching, and classroom experience. Here boredom is akin to indifference, and antithetical to the promotion of peace. Marnie speaks of the need for more fun in life, and in the classroom. Johanna talks of creating a happy place, where children can figure out what their dreams are and get support for pursuing and realizing them. John (6/24/11) considers:

> I guess the way you'd [a teacher] help them [students] is by having somebody to talk to them, having them have playtime a little bit. Not a lot of kids get playtime on their block...and ask everybody and help everybody.

Marnie (6/24/11) imagines pedagogy for peace in this way:

> Peace drawings on the wall, stuff like that, I would let kids express themselves...write words everywhere...papers with messages, like "keep trying" and post all over the school... inquiry, and like, in this classroom, community, teaching as asking questions, letting the children express themselves.... Group things, like what they feel about that....

There is, then, among these students the idea that teaching for peace involves having help and being helped to affirm their own subjectivity, thought, experience, and emotion in freedom and joy; and learning to freely give such to others, from this place to "think of ways we can stop violence" (Marnie, 6/24/11), "make a difference," and "give back" (Johanna, 6/24/11) as well. Desire and ethics, herein, while often experientially at odds, seem also ultimately ever interminably intertwined and interconnected, and requisites to address for realizing peace.

In offering a small window here into the work undertaken with these students in two New York City elementary classrooms, I have sought to present, as well, a glimpse into the peace profiles emerging within each classroom, and through such, a consideration of the possible ways in which the pedagogical pursuit of peace, and against violence, in each class may also have impacted the perspectives on and practices for peace these students take up. The first-graders, in concert with the peace curriculum they are taught, for instance, are most committed to and oriented around the work of giving peace and making peace, as individuals and together, each in his or her own shared and different ways. Similarly, immersed in their curricular inquiry into violence, the fourth-graders each and all express a strong attunement to the presence of violence in their lives, communities, and world, and interest in and insights into its causes and the paths by which they can stop violence at its source—even as individually some of their responses differ from one another in manifold ways too.

In this approach, I trust I have neither marginalized nor minimized the voice of each child, as I have also sought to attend to the presentation of each and their ideas in their uniqueness and singularity, pointing to at least some of the ways in which lived experience and subjectivity are powerfully at work in any pursuit of peace, and response to pedagogy aimed at such. More broadly, in working with and listening to and reflecting upon the contributions of these students, I have sought, in some small way, to explore the views and visions of children concerning peace and educating for peace—to "begin with children," toward gleaning new and renewing dreams of and dreaming for peace among us, as we dialogue together; and pedagogical possibilities in the way of their realization. In the concluding chapter to follow, bearing something of the imprint of such gleaning, I seek to hopefully inspire the reader to such, and much more beyond.

Chapter 7
On Re-Imagining Peace and Pedagogies for Peace

Gandhi (1942/2007) specifically points out that the nonviolence movement is "not a program of seizure of power" but a "program of transformation of relationships" (p. 40).

-Ghandi (cited in Wang, in press, p. 17)

We find in every school in which we have worked, the most frequently raised issue is relationships.

-Poplin, 1999, p. 31

The first peace, which is the most important, is that which comes within the souls of people when they realize their relationship, their oneness with the universe and all its powers.

-Black Elk (cited in Pedersen, 2007, p. 3)

On Being and Becoming Peace, Pedagogically

I began this book with an excerpt from the words of Vietnamese Buddhist monk and peace activist Thich Nhat Hanh (1987/1996) on *Being Peace*. In it, he spoke of our world as being like a small boat upon stormy seas. He spoke of our propensity to panic, feeling most small, and vulnerable, and even despairing, amid the alarming currents of injustice, and if not violence itself, the perpetual threat of it in the face of the massive arsenals of nuclear (and chemical) weapons waiting at the ready throughout the world. We ourselves, he also reminds, have become the greatest threat, a very dangerous species: tiny and tossed, terrified, and yet also terrifying. His response, then, not at once a call to nuclear disarmament, directs us rather first to the fount of ourselves, to a kind of disarmament of ourselves and of our relationships. Seemingly so simple—and perhaps, we might at first surmise, overly simplistic—he asks us each to sit still, stay calm, smile, and walk with serenity. For, in such lucidity, he claims, comes knowledge and action that can save many. Not at all simple or simplistic, how I engage here with myself matters—and you with yourself, with the wild overwhelming waters, with others in this fragile boat we are all in together. From Thich Nhat Hanh, we are told that you are, and I am—each of us is—called to be, can be, that calm in the storm.

Education, especially via the institution of schooling, is a very small boat indeed, and in which perhaps the most vulnerable among us abide: children and youth, with their teachers,[1] and others. Herein, too, they are at and about this human project intentionally together, involving knowledge and action indeed in the way of a kind of salvation: what Freire (1970/1993) has called "our historical vocation of humanization" and "radical love" in a world of oppression, injustice, and violence; and Arendt (1954/1993), our responsibility to the new in our midst, and in love of the world, for together "renewing a common world" (p. 196). Such is a project, presumably too, of hope, and not horror, for human potential and peace, singularly and in solidarity, and for the world we share—central to which are our relations and ways of relating therein.

Yet, horror there is, horrors there are—from growing educational inequities and widening achievement gaps that serve to further minoritize and impoverish many, foreclosing life chances and opportunities, to mass school shootings of the young even against the young; for instance, in the U.S., political control of schooling and education here through a coalition involving government and business interests has also compelled the "gracious submission" (Pinar, 2012) of teachers and students (and administrators, parents, and education professors, perhaps among others) to a high-stakes testing regime that significantly reduces what it means to educate and be educated—that is, minimizing the import and role of culture, and context, and human singularity and subjectivity, in knowledge, growth, and understanding; flattening educational experience and meaningful engagement in teaching and learning; and undermining the cultivation of supportive relationship and community amid conditions of competition, surveillance, and accountability from a "bottom-line" conception of success and achievement as measured on tests privileging only that which is measurable, preset, and deter-

---

1 Pinar (2012) and Taubman (2009) have discussed this growing vulnerability, particularly respecting teachers in the U.S. in the contemporary context.

mined in advance, and not at all involving or by those (teachers and students, among others) engaged in the actual educational process and project, and thereby also evaluated.

Such a situation clearly, too, flies in the face of academic freedom and freedom of thought, genuine dialogue and inquiry, and informed praxis and social action emerging from such—treasured ideals and essential tenets of a democratic society, central to human agency. Pinar (2004) even draws upon the historical case of the Weimar Republic and its lapse in Germany as an analogy, or perhaps caution-ary tale, for our present condition, in education, and in relation more broadly to society^2 and the world at large. While perhaps pressing such an analogy too far, I am reminded too of what Arendt (2006) calls the "banality of evil" via her analysis of Eichmann's (and others') role in the horrors and Holocaust enacted by the Nazis. Easier to cast simply as a monster (or monsters, sociopaths, etc.), Eichmann (and other S.S. perpetrators) conducted himself (themselves) rather in a normalized manner, as bureaucrat(s) and servant(s) of the State, carrying out orders, his (their) work, to the best of his ability (their abilities). For Arendt, it was and is this relinquishing of thought, and thinking—foundational to human freedom and conscience—that made and makes such evil possible, and at its most dangerous.

In the least, at present, panic may be becoming one of our norms (or anesthetizing substances and solutions)—clearly an obstacle to lucid thinking and thought; we are tempted to panic, to cultivate panic, tossed about by many and turbulent waters, and alas so much is of our own dangerous making. Schools, administrators, and teach-ers especially, are increasingly tormented by exponential accusations and expectations—held accountable for this presumed abysmal state of affairs located in crisis, and for delivering us from it, for saving us all. Educators somehow are to blame for such forces rocking us all about, and are called to tame the waters, walk on water, or make a better boat for dry land. Such says nothing of the forces and waters

---

2 Naomi Wolf (2007), in analyzing the changes in American society beside the documented course of development of governments that became totalitarian, identifies seven of ten categories through which the U.S. has moved and is moving in such a direction.

herein threatening to overwhelm, pressing upon and inordinately pressuring, parents, families, and children especially, either.

Yet, while we certainly can and in many ways must consider disarmament of such an educational system, and reconstitution of its internal and external institutional relations, we might turn first to that which Hanh (1987/1996) entreats us: ourselves as educators (as scholars, teachers, teachers of teachers, parents, fellow humans, etc.), and the relationships we tame, walk or make, emulate, create and cultivate. We might hearken, too, to Arendt's (1954/1993) reminder of our responsibility in and to such relationships—toward past and future, as well as the present; to the new in our midst and the world in which we dwell, as well as to ourselves. We each are small indeed, yet not utterly powerless in the face of all we encounter, and ever connected to the great largesse beyond. Victor Frankl (1946/1997), the psychiatrist who survived a Nazi concentration camp during World War II and sought to glean insight into human being from such a dire context, speaks of what he calls the last of human freedoms, choosing one's response even to such dehumanization and in such suffering. As a popular contemporary teacher, Carolyn Myss (2004), whose work is rooted in comparative religion and spirituality as well as intuitive and integrated medicine, discusses such in terms of acts of power: the moment-by-moment choice we each are afforded to empower or "grace" ourselves and others, or to disempower or "disgrace" ourselves and others.

I engage these ideas and thoughts here to highlight a key emergent emphasis, for me, from this study, which seems somewhat foundational to any consideration of reimagining peace and pedagogies for peace toward efforts of realizing peace among us and in our world: that involving *the import of attention to and inquiry into and transformation of our relationships themselves*. Such relationships include those we have with and toward power—including our own, as much as the powers that be—and posture toward peace, and the power of peace in human life. In education and specifically in teaching, Poplin (1999) highlights the centrality of relationships, their profound and defining influence, and yet how little they are explicitly recognized, attended, or fruitfully and faithfully engaged—even as they also often present the most challenges, and even obstacles to peace as lived, and educational fruitfulness. Mindful of avoiding a repetition of "find-ings" or insights presented in former chapters, then, while hopefully in some synthesizing ways embracing them, in this chapter I seek to conclude this work with some initial engagement with and considera-tion of this central address.

Echoing something of the rich historical framing embodied in the symbology of peace—from ancient origins found simply in the image of three circles within a larger circle to demonstrate what has been conceptualized as the triune and transcendent nature of life (that is, embracing past, present, future; art, science, and religion)—I also do so here, mindful of three key interconnected and mutually constitu-tive relations therein, that with: self/ourselves, other/others, and world(s) in which we dwell. These relationships I also take up in concert with corresponding attention to mind, heart, and body; embracing time, space, place—the dynamic context in which self meets self and other and world, or such come together. While impact-ed largely by what I have gleaned from study of the visions and voices of the student teachers, teachers, and children with whom I have worked through this project, I also make an effort to make mention of related scholarship in peace education and on peace as respecting curriculum and pedagogy, in the way of elucidating common considerations and/or introducing differing ones, as well as enriching and deepening such exploration in my discussion concern-ing our dreams of peace and educational efforts toward the aspira-tional living out of them. Additionally, my attention here, given the nature of my study, and interest at work in initiating it, as well as address taken up with participants herein, is admittedly focused on subjectivity, and this first and primary relationship of self to and with self—and directed and mindful intention concerning such—albeit ever formed and informed by that with others in a world, and pro-foundly affecting such as well.

Peace, Pedagogy, and Self: Becoming "A Person Who Is a Person"

At the start of this work, I reflected a little upon my own heart for peace—and my thinking about and writing of it—at a coffeehouse in New York, amid the sounds of Christmas music, meeting also memories of childhood, hearkening to moments and meanings of peace rooted in my own history and experience, my own subjectivity—and my beloved uncle's annual performance by which he resoundingly proclaimed: "Let there be peace on earth, and let it begin with me." Now it is again fall, sounds of the season playing, in another coffee-house, where I seek to write and think and reflect upon peace, and as informed by this study, and the journey I have taken in the course of it. However, I am no longer far from home—in fact, back in my native Louisiana, the past and childhood palpably with me and most pre-sent, as I strive to offer care and support to my elderly parents, my mom nearly wholly immobile and beyond speech, and Dad, legally blind. Here—even as I am filled with far too much care concerning myself, in the aftermath of much, an experience of a kind of totalizing loss involving home and work and myriad relations, and before a future of profound uncertainty—I seek to pen what I have learned of peace, and possibility for teaching peace.

Helen Keller, perhaps critical of a well-cited appeal to faith con-cerning peace from the Christian Bible, asserts: "I do not want the peace that passeth understanding. I want the understanding which bringeth peace" (cited in Lichtenstein, 1962). Through this work, and in my own life, I have indeed sought such understanding and to illuminate potentialities for its pedagogical cultivation among us, and yet also experienced, at times, this peace which exceeds understand-ing, well beyond me and my own capacity to comprehend. I have also, and do, especially now so much more than I should wish, struggle for such understanding, and for that which uncannily lies beyond it as well—in this, and now, I falter, and ask: *How can I, then, speak here of peace? Can I still submit the import of subjectivity herein, and try to exclude my own (sticking only to the gleanings from teachers and children, or the literature perhaps), and given my own present subjective case and place?* And then I remember, with King's (cited in Carson, 2000, p. 170) reminder that peace is not the absence of tension, that neither peace, nor understanding, are easy; finding perhaps each its own felt presence and work, and deepest and most abiding meaning and significance, in contexts seemingly antithetical to and conditions at odds with such. In this, there is an ongoing call and commitment required of each of us, something to ever be achieved or accomplished, and from the site of our own subjectivity.

In a lecture I attended, Naomi Tutu (2013), South African human rights advocate and daughter of Archbishop Desmond Tutu, spoke about "Ubuntu: The Challenge of Being Human." With humor and heart, she related some of the many proverbs and sayings taught her by her parents, a central one of which can be translated to say: "That person is a person who is a person." Such a declaration constitutes the highest of praise, recognizing that such a one is aware of and apprehends the responsibility of being and becoming fully human, reaches for and realizes his or her highest humanity, well at the work of truly achieving his or her personhood. This mindfulness, work and even struggle, expresses, to me, something of the heart of this way in which by and to the path of peace we are called to relate anew, and perhaps differently, to ourselves, to self, and the ongoing project of being and becoming who we are and wish to be.

"I have not the shadow of a doubt that any man or woman can achieve what I have, if he or she would make the same effort and cultivate the same hope and faith," claims Gandhi (cited in Wang, in press, p. 1), whose "experiments with truth," as he named them, were undertaken in the laboratory of his own personhood, and embodied existence, and have inspired so many to the call of peace and nonviolence. Herein, he speaks of achievement, effort, and cultivation, and elsewhere of the development of inner discipline through spiritual awareness, learning to overcome fear, and seeking in his thoughts, words, and actions to ever respond nonviolently. Wang, who draws upon Gandhi in her work in proposing that we take up nonviolence[3] as at the heart of our educational vision, via the internationalization of curriculum studies specifically, speaks of nonviolence as not only "fundamentally an educational project" (p. 8), but also "a way of living life" and "a particular mode of strength."

---

3 Wang (in press) prefers a focus on nonviolence rather than peace, as such draws attention to a worldwide political movement, and a historical and contemporary stance against and denouncement of all forms of violence. Such is also a concept underdeveloped and unaddressed in education, by and large.

Consciously Cultivating Subjects of Peace and Personhood

For peace, as for teaching peace, it would seem, the self, one's relation to and with the self, the development of self in relation to such an aim and mode and way, must be taken up as an educational project, perhaps at the core of, fundamental to, the educational project itself writ large—gleaned from Thich Nhat Hanh's (1987/1996) focus on the person that is you, and me, as source and site of peace, with which I began this work; to study of the lives of champions of peace (like Hanh or Gandhi, 1958) or of advocates of peace (like Aurobindo, 1993; or Krishnamurti, 1996) rooted in inner transformation and inward journey; to the experiential insights here of teachers and aspiring teachers and young students: emphasizing lived, personal and consciously, vividly, experienced experience, the need to actually *be* peace and to pursue and choose it consciously; and speaking much, if only indirectly, of the power of agency and identification—with peace as peacemakers, or alternately with violence as bullies or gang members.

Historical understandings and endorsements of this central educational address, at least concerning attention to the self, also abound: for example, from the Western tradition alone, much is made of Socrates' edict to "know thyself," and child-centered progressives have continually emphasized the work of self-understanding and development. More recent mainstream concerns such as about reflective practice on the part of teachers allude to this claim, as do those about student self-assessment, though generally they are framed through imposed and disembodied purposes not issuing from teachers or student themselves, nor aspiring to the achievement of personhood. In the present educational moment, in such the personhood of the teacher is actually disavowed, and that of kids as well, in contexts of standardization wherein interests of a global economy are dominant. Criticism is brought to this case and condition, as well, in the peace education literature (Reardon & Snauwaert, 2011), and the significance of subjectivity, one's relation with oneself, brought to bear, if only sometimes indirectly, in such as well.

Sharon Chubbuck and Michalinos Zembylas (2011) consider the various theories of and facets constituting violence in seeking to articulate a theoretical model of a critical pedagogy for nonviolence. Here, they highlight from Johan Galtung (1990) those circumstances (that is, direct, structural, cultural) that deprive the human being of his or her own life potential; and in their developing framework endorse a holistic integrated way of life beginning *from the inside* (emphasis mine), involving too what they call "critical emotional praxis," rooted in the recognition of the powerful role emotions play in cultivating peace, or getting in the way of such (Chubbuck & Zembylas, 2011). Wang (in press) similarly calls for attending to nonviolence as a "whole being experience" (p. 24), inclusive of deep and important emotional work, and the renewal of human imagination, as well. She maintains that:

> An educational project of nonviolence involves intellectual, emotional, social, and spiritual cultivation of personhood situated in history and culture... (p. 9)

Many scholars in the arena of critical peace education (for example, Bajaj & Brantmeier, 2011; Chubbuck & Zembylas, 2011; Hantzopoulos, 2011; Reardon, 2013; Trifonas & Wright, 2013), both in reviewing the peace education literature and in setting forth that deemed to be vital tenets of such education, relatedly assert the import of individually as well as collectively promoting: critical consciousness, alternative nonviolent imagining, avenues of empowerment, oppositional as well as transformational and participatory agency, and creative and renewing action and reflection. Such affirmations, as matters for research and teaching, also emphasize the messy, complex, particular, and personal ways these aims are and must ever be taken up in local contexts and cultures, issuing from unique and dynamic struggles against violence, and for peace, human rights, and fullness of life.

This significance of one's own project of personhood—relation to oneself and one's own course, including ethics, emotion, desire, and destiny—concerning peace and pedagogy for peace that I am hoping to emphasize, with the support of other scholarship herein, is illuminated well, for example, via one such context explored in the study of Chubbuck and Zembylas (2011) involving a novice teacher committed to educating for peace and nonviolence in an urban school in the

Midwestern U.S. This teacher found, and these scholars found from and with her, that an essential challenge for and claim upon her in this commitment was that of nonviolence toward herself, and in all of her relations, and in such modeling for and instructing each child in the same.

The teachers, and aspiring teachers, in my study echo this emphasis in gleaning that in deep and abiding ways you teach who you are (Aoki, 2005)—peace, and teaching, quintessentially involving subjective labor; that not only for peace in their own lives, but also for teaching it, it becomes necessary to personally pursue peace, to aim at being and becoming peace oneself, and enacting and initiating such in one's work with students. The students seem, too, to concur on this point in their attention to the import of voice, choice, belonging, recognition, discovery, agency, and growth in experiencing and identifying with peace and the work of peace in the world. Herein is a person-centered purpose and pedagogy, oriented around the achievement and cultivation of personhood, and human flourishing—encompassing harmonious means and ends, and dreams and ongoing dreaming of peace.

What if we undertook as an intentional human project this full-bodied, whole being, and experiential cultivation of personhood as foundational and central to education? In the aftermath of the tragic killings at the elementary school in Newtown, Connecticut, President Barack Obama (2012) addressed the nation and those so personally suffering such trauma and grieving and loss: in his address, reporting that "among the fallen were also teachers, men and women who devoted their lives to helping children fulfill their dreams." Here he explicitly acknowledges human dreams, the fulfillment of human potential, as at the heart of the work of education, and teaching. Among scholars, too, it is understood as well as uncovered that amid life in school, or other educational institutions, with their routines and rituals, and via an oft-hidden curriculum,[4] as well as or in contradiction to the explicit one, the self is profoundly in the making; and one's

---

4 While a good deal of contemporary attention has been given to the hidden curriculum, Philip Jackson (1968/1990) first coined the term in his analysis of life in classrooms, and that which is implicitly and indirectly taught therein, even if not a part of the official or formal curriculum of study.

relation to, ideals for, posture toward, etc., one's self; and one's own history, experience, development, and future—potential, dreams and their realization (for example, Blumenfeld-Jones, 2012; Ladson-Billings, 2009; Pinar, 2012; Wexler, 1992). Yet, even also in such—including compelling criticism brought to bear on the dominance of the instrumental, even inanimate/in-animating, maintained in educational policy, discourse, and practice—this important making of the self, and purposeful cultivation of personhood, is in the main-stream still largely marginalized, ignored, dismissed, or outright opposed (Davies, 2006; Sonu, 2013).

Any response to this question I have posed must certainly, of course too, remain incomplete and inconclusive, open and ongoing—an enduring human question and response to be existentially and experientially ever undertaken and taken up. Yet, here, I can try to but mention briefly a direction, potential directions, for such as gleaned from the insights of those I have had the privilege of seeing with and hearing from via this study—in the least prodding each reader to dream peace anew for herself or himself, to attend and pursue peace in his or her own person, in the making of the curriculum of his or her own life, pedagogically inspiring self and others herein as well. For as Wang (in press) so aptly puts it: "If we intentionally cultivate nonviolence to its full potential, the world [too] will become more nonviolent and loving" (p. 4). Such necessarily centers on taking seriously the challenge of being fully human, the achievement of one's own personhood, which is also inherently attending the wholeness and fullness of one's own being. Herein, then, I relate these considerations primarily through the call of intention—education already quite enamored with goal-making processes[5]—and yet attuned to the need for a kind of triune address of wholeness and personhood involving mind, heart, and body, and self with others in a world; wherein implications for teacher education and development mirror in foundational ways articulating and enacting pedagogies for peace with children in schools as well.

---

5 Wang (in press) highlights another triad, concerning the intention of cultivating personhood and nonviolence via the curriculum, endorsing an integrated address involving purpose, content, and means.

Mind Matters in Matters of Peace and Pedagogy for Peace

To speak of education as an intentional human project, to speak of intention itself, is to attune oneself to the work and power of the mind, in human life and society, and perhaps our faith in such as well.

> As a man thinketh so is he.
> > Proverbs 23:7
> The unexamined life is not worth living.
> > Socrates
> What you focus on expands.
> Thought creates emotion creates action creates reality.
> A mind too active is no mind at all.

Nearly innumerable traditions, theories, and studies attest to the import of the mind in all we perceive, experience, say, do, and affect. Education has historically been focused herein as well—via the development of the intellect and focus on mastery in academic disciplines of study, and even now, in the U.S. and elsewhere, in the overwhelmingly pervasive and obsessive establishment of specific and sanctioned, largely cognitive, goals, and evaluation processes and surveillance mechanisms seeking to ensure their realization. Yet, in many ways, as conceived and cultivated, such approaches often actually miss "mind," "minding the mind," or mindfulness not actually considered in relation to all this epistemological intention.

Concerning peace, then, and as but a beginning, teachers (and aspiring), and with their students, might take up the explicit study of mind, their own minds, and here particularly concerning peace, its absence, opposite, obstacles to, and agents for such therein. Such includes attention to thought, their own thoughts and consideration of where particular thoughts come from, what they affect, and where they lead, as well as inquiry into their "truth" or partiality. This call is not unrelated to Freire's (1970/1993) notion of "conscientization," aimed at cultivating awareness of one's situation and attitude in and thoughts about it; Greene's (1995/2000) call to "wide-awakeness"; or the autobiographical work of critical self-examination of one's identity and social location advocated and practiced by many in teacher education (for example, Genor & Goodwin, 2005; Sleeter, 2005), as well as that more full-bodied subjectively emergent approach of Pinar (2012) via *currere*.[6] Yet, it also might be inclusive of varied and sundry theories of mind and mind/mindfulness practices—and of the imagination and its cultivation, from academic arts and sciences to ancient wisdom traditions, and engaged broadly in the full pursuit of personhood, and what that might mean, as well as its pedagogical cultivation, and in terms of nonviolence and peace—and particularly in one's lived experience and context. Systematically taking this address up in teacher education and professional development, and via curriculum and pedagogy for children of various grades and ages and educational contents and contexts, is clearly possible though neither singular nor subject to any fixed or standard prescription; nor is it simple, involving memory, imagination and moment-by-moment interpretation of thought and experience.[7]

Those in this study—both adults and children discussing peace as a state of being and also as a state of mind, wherein consciousness figures largely—in this regard, for example, speak of learning to change one's mind, stepping back, listening, reminding, and paying attention. There is the articulation that simply being invited to think about peace in their own lives, whether through photography or other engagement, and reflectively talk or write about such gives them a clearer understanding of what peace means and how they might dream, commit to, and cultivate it. Some, in relation to mind, actively advocate meditation, solitude or retreat, such as via the peace corner. Others mention drawing, journaling or writing down their own thoughts, to quell mental turmoil in some cases, and for taking their thoughts themselves as objects of study and understanding. Also, though not generally the terminology used, many also advised the promotion of "beginner's mind" (a Buddhist concept, see Hanh,

---

6 *Currere*—taken from the Latin infinitive of the word *curriculum*, meaning "to run" in drawing attention to the experience of the student or one running the course of study—is an autobiographical method designed and forwarded by Pinar (2012), originally with Madeleine Grumet in the 1970s, to elucidate the educational meaning and subjective significance issuing from engagement with curriculum.

7 The study of the mind and practice of contemplation, and related addresses, and as concerning the work of teaching and project of education, for example, have been taken up in and from the work of Linda Lantieri (2002), and via the Garrison Institute, as well, in large measure, devoted to such.

1992): openness and expansiveness of mind, and critical questioning, through exposure to various mind-changing activities and multiple perspectives via curriculum and teaching. Actively visualizing and imaginatively dreaming peace is affirmed among these participants as well.

Jan Bernard (2013), co-founder of Gift of Goals, has described a goal as being "thought magnified," mind transfixed to some aim or desire. As much as education as conceived and enacted is inscribed in goals, little thought is perhaps actually given to such as a matter of mind, or in relation to self. Despite subjection to predominantly goals- and outcomes-oriented education via schooling, according to Bernard, research on goal setting and achievement[8] among the adult American population actually found that most participants— something near 80%—didn't see themselves as genuinely having or setting goals for their lives, and yet that those who do and write them down are nine times more likely to achieve what they want, their dream or version of success, in life. Bernard also draws upon the work of Sheryl Sandberg, CEO of Facebook, who has made the case, too, that genuine ambition in any pursuit requires the unique charting of one's own course[9] in alignment with one's values and dreams, and fitting one's life and way of living: doing what one loves, the key to success.

Relatedly, then—in concert with the attention the pre-service and practicing teachers and elementary students here give to the import for peace and for teaching it of such things as self-knowledge and self-expression; choice, voice, agency, and efficacy; meaning, growth, and sense of accomplishment and fulfillment; and finding and doing and pursuing what one loves and enjoys, the happy life of one's dreams—teachers and students in their education might be brought into relationship again and again not only with this lifelong, living

---

8 Bernard (2013) draws upon the research here out of Virginia Tech on goals, particularly that of Professor Emeritus David Kohl, as well as through the Ford Foundation.

9 Herein is an interesting resonance with curriculum, involving not only a course of study to be taken but also the experience of taking such a course—and the assertion that one's subjective agency in choosing and charting such a course is not at all inconsequential.

goal brought before them concerning the challenge of being fully human, cultivating each his or her own highest personhood; but also with goals in themselves as themselves, for consideration, and in relation to mind, their minds, and the work of peace particularly herein, as well as in their lives and the dreams they have for them. What possibilities might emerge if goals were taken up in this way in universities, schools, classrooms and curricula, with teachers and students, via teaching and learning? If the academic goals we set in the disciplines sought kinship with such? If at least some of our goals meaningfully emerged in the context of educational living together, some singular and some shared, and in the way of these directions that make for peace as lived, and desirable—teachers and students figuring out their own goals, and collective ones, and the ways in which education may illuminate, expand, and transform them, as well as contribute to their realization?

Participants in this study made much of the possibilities of free play and exploration, choice time, problem- and project-based learning, inquiries emerging from the interests, issues, and questions of students and teachers, singularly and together. Discovery via study and investigation, experimentation and learning, was also identified as a source of pleasure and peace—the mind expanded, knowing itself to be growing and gaining new understanding. Mention was made also of the import of celebrating and showcasing and sharing the fruits of one's explorations and engagements—one's own developing powers, of expressing and sharing thoughts and ideas; and listening to, receiving, and embracing such from others too. Herein are goals emerging in the course of meaningful living, loving, and learning, playing and purposing, together—much as John Dewey (1938) and William E. Doll, Jr. (1993) speak of them, worthy aims issuing authentically from lived experience and the dynamic, changing, rarely-predictable-in-advance purposes presenting themselves therein.

Such reminds me of, and resonates with, Pinar's (2012) conviction that education be transformative, concerning the mobilization of self toward self and social reconstruction. In this, curriculum and pedagogy involves the pursuit of understanding from the site of each student's, and teacher's, subjectivity, temporality, and lived experience; wherein meaning is made in study of and conversation with, in relation to and relating to, subject matter and social context. Elsewhere, Pinar (2009) speaks of the cultivation of passionate lives for and in public service. James Macdonald (1995) considers the task of education relatedly as well to be what he calls "centering": our aspirations reaching out and up toward "the completion of the person or the creation of meaning that utilizes all the potential given to each person" (p. 87). Others, like Nel Noddings (2005), and the Dalai Lama (1999), ask us thus to rethink education itself around the aims of happiness, and care (that is, for self, others, the world, ideas)— integrally tied to peace and personhood, and pedagogically so too. Such, clearly, are matters of the mind, and yet of the heart, most certainly, as well. As goal guru, Bernard (2013) urges one to ask of any intention to which she or he has set his or her mind: *Does it make my heart sing?*

Peace, Pedagogy, and Other(s):
Becoming "A Person Who Is a Person through Others"

Frederick Beuchner (1991), in *Now and Then: A Memoir of Vocation*, suggests that our heart can only truly sing when we seek to aspire to and actualize the place where our deep gladness meets the world's deep need. Thich Nhat Hanh (1987/1996) has spoken here to us from the start of the peace that can save many lives, beginning with our own presence amid others in calmness and smiling. I initiated this work hoping to cultivate my own heart for peace, and for pedagogically promoting the work of peace with children through those who teach them with whom I work. Questions that guided me in such work, and with which I challenged my students as pre-service teachers, included: How might we connect our own personal struggles with the struggles of others and the pain of the world? Through such, how might education be taken up as an avenue for freedom, fellowship, and healing—a site to inspire and enable us to become participants in creating a more just, joyous, compassionate, and beautiful world? Yet, from my experience as well as from research (for example, Puigvert, 2010), I realized that desire and ethics oft fail to meet:

that amid the alluring force of domination or violence—especially within contexts where individual competition, achievement, and satisfaction are dominant endorsements, and agency is largely thwarted and powerlessness deeply felt—care for others and the call of the just and good are all too easily marginalized, abnegated, or dismissed.

Herein, efforts must be made to reach and transform the heart, our relationship to our own desires as well as to others; to unite and unify mind and heart, as well as self with others. For, the second saying of Ubuntu, according to Naomi Tutu (2013), essential and integral to the first concerning the "person who is a person," is this: "A person is a person through others." We can only know and realize our humanity, develop personhood, realize peace, in relationship with others, engaging the heart—the other as one with self, as brother, as sister, and fellow human, even the other known to be and experienced as enemy, such as in the context of apartheid in South Africa to which the healing aspirations of Ubuntu were brought by Archbishop Desmond Tutu and others. As philosopher Jacques Derrida (1985) articulates, in explorations of autobiography via what he calls *"oto"-biography* (of the "ear") and *"autre"-biography* (pertaining to that which is "other"), our sense of self comes in and through relationship to the other—it is the ear of the other in fact who signs our name. To know peace, to intend peace, to teach peace, to actualize peace, we must embrace the heart, the other, others, in love.

Embracing the Need for Love, to Love, and the "Unity of Life"

Eric Fromm (1956/2006)—social psychologist, psychoanalyst, and philosopher affiliated with the critical work of the Frankfurt School—makes the claim that love is "the answer to the problem of modern existence" (p. 7). From this classic work *The Art of Loving*, he explores what such means as the only fulfilling and fully affirming response to our deepest human need—"to overcome our separateness, to leave the prison of our aloneness" (p. 9). In such, too, is a moving forward toward a new harmony, a human one—harmony, often a term used to define peace itself, as well.

Alas, in the realm of education, though, we speak little of love, and historically, the work of education has done much to cultivate rather than overcome separation and alienation. For example, abiding legacies and commitments that sever reason from emotion, mind from body, objectivity from subjectivity, and privilege the former (i.e., reason, mind, objectivity) over the latter (i.e., emotion, body, subjectivity) contribute to this case. From one realm are the influences of objectivism, positivism, and atomism through philosophy and the sciences. Through the advent of industrialization, Fordism, and the specialization and division of labor, the factory model for schooling, a strong affinity for social efficiency, and separate disciplines, subject periods, grades, etc., come to frame and form educational thought and practice. And the productivity sought and affirmed herein generally has little to do with human solidarity, community, or connection—or the heart.

Freire (1970/1993) critiques what he calls this "banking model" of education, rooted in colonial dehumanization, where students themselves are not engaged as human subjects, but rather as objects to be acted upon, to be filled with the established knowledge prescribed. Such also fails in authentically engaging teacher and student interest or desire as well, divorced from context, culture, and conditions as lived. For Gandhi (1958), all forms of violence are rooted in this work of separation—of self from other(s), of human life from other living beings in the world—which violates the essential truth of "the unity of life." Arguing for education, curriculum, and pedagogy grounded in the principle and cause of nonviolence, Wang (in press) articulates this idea through the truth of interconnectedness—to which she reminds that contemporary science and manifold cultural and wisdom traditions bear witness. Such must entail addressing a deep-seated dualism, particularly in the West, and its corresponding logic of control and dominance (Doll, 1993; Quinn, 2001). Peace education itself has also been described in terms of transformational processes oriented around the centrality of human relationships, in countering such divisions; to promote cultures of peace (for example, Navarro-Castro & Nario-Galace, 2008); and involving critically challenging and changing relations of power (Reardon, 2000) "into productive, positive expressions that promote social justice..." (Chubbuck & Zembylas, 2011, p. 272).

In this sense, though perhaps the project of education has been dominantly framed more around violence than peace (for example, Gemstone Peace Education Team, 2008; Sonu, 2013; Wang, in press), and implicated in the perpetuation of violence—systemic, structural, cultural, and psychic (Asher, 2009), if not direct; there have been and are also a cloud of witnesses herein testifying to that which might make for peace, and such via curriculum and pedagogy, in challenging violence and cultivating nonviolence; and this, concerning reconciling and bringing people together, if not in love, then at least in solidarity. Not only from what has already been mentioned—for example, the Dalai Lama (1999) on education for happiness, well-being, and compassion; Noddings (2005) on orienting curriculum around care for self, others, ideas, the world; and Freire (1970/1993) on conscientization, dialogue, problem-posing, and praxis—but also in a great body of literature beyond, we find this heart, such as in the areas of human rights, critical multiculturalism, cosmopolitanism, democratic global citizenship, anti-oppressive education, culturally relevant pedagogy, peace education, holistic education, and more. What if we drew upon the collective wisdom of such traditions together, and brought them into conversation, too, to support the further pedagogical advancement of peace?

What is shared herein, and in other such work, is an attention to this notion of the other, and otherness, and the call to embrace diversity, difference, hospitality, and inclusion; and come together in and through such, for healing, forgiveness, empowerment, and transformation in genuine listening,[10] learning and dialogic engagement, toward the task of renewing a common world we can love, in which we can nonviolently, even lovingly, relate and together share— enriched and enhanced by such relations. Such includes addressing

---

10 For beginning directions in literature of note in education, curriculum, and pedagogy on the somewhat lesser explored directions here of hospitality and forgiveness, see bibliographies in Quinn (2009, 2010). The burgeoning scholarship being undertaken herein on listening (e.g., Garrison, 2011) is drawn upon toward the engagement of personhood, morally and for democracy, from a Buddhist lens, as well, in Shi/Leong (in progress).

cultures of, and our own, unconsciousness; the recognition of "codes of power" (Delpit, 2006) and asymmetrical power relations (Bajaj, 2008); and adopting what Joe Kincheloe (2002) has called "power literacy"—through critical engagement with others (Bajaj & Brantmeier, 2011) and with counter-narratives to dominant ways of knowing and accounts of knowledge. Yet, this work also embraces study of (by teachers and students) what Wang (in press) describes as that which "belongs to the vital, life-affirmative, and best part of each culture and may have the potentiality to unite us across differences to co-create together more compassionate and creative expressions of humanity" (pp. 9–10). What curriculum and pedagogy might emerge, how might education and schools be transformed, and personhood and peace be cultivated, if such study was seriously taken up and taken seriously?

Maria Hantzopoulos (2011), in setting forth a case study wherein critical peace education has effectually been institutionalized in a public school via a comprehensive approach, here warns against the demonization of the public sphere to which we may fall prey in critical reproductive analyses of schools and educational institutions, and societies, as sites simply of oppression and inequity. Of this case, she speaks of the participatory nature of intentional school structures (for example, prep central, advisory, town hall, fairness committee, co-constructed curriculum) that worked to mobilize and satisfy among those in the school, particularly students, "a *hunger* for real democratization" (emphasis mine—desire, p. 228, citing McGinn, 1996, p. 342), which not only supported student achievement but also agency, and an understanding of democracy. Dewey (1916), seeking a democratic conception of education, sets forth these criteria: "How numerous and varied are the interests which are consciously shared? How full and free is the interplay with other forms of association?" (p. 87). Deep peace, deep democracy, entails in this way ongoing and manifold encounters with others, in difference; and through such, cultivating shared interests and new affiliations—what students, aspiring teachers, and teachers in this study spoke of as "unity-in-diversity." "Peace is not a discrete event," then, as Wang reminds (in press), "but a process of daily engagement in democratic life" (p. 7), wherein "every community becomes an important site for enacting nonviolent dynamics" (p. 6).

It is clear that the development of personhood for peace thus engages, as has been discussed, critical emotional work (Chubbuck & Zembylas, 2011), the heart, desire, and ethics—a person who is a person through, and with, and in relation to, others. Participants in this peace study, in this way, demonstrate in their peace photos and speak of the need to seek, find, pursue, and do what one loves *with* those one loves. Herein is the work of discovering avocation, meaningfully and pleasurably developing one's emerging powers, with others, in a community of care, belonging, contribution, respect, responsibility, and joy. The heart of the matter truly becomes: "How might we best differ for one another?" (Hershock, 2009, p. 160); and as we live and learn together, in care for one another?

The truth of the "unity of life" seems, too, to be affirmed by them in emphases not only on community as curriculum, responsive pedagogy, and genuine engagement wherein no fixed outcomes can truly apply; but also on the need for addressing aggressive impulse, conflict, and suffering and injustice concerning such issues as relating to divisions of gender, race, and class—and concretely, in images of hunger, homelessness, violence, poverty, and environmental degradation. Expressed is a need for connection and interconnectedness—via working and playing and talking together, and in efforts at integrating meaningfully past, present, and future; home and school; and the myriad and oft oppositional forces of living. The first-graders engage and endorse certain classroom practices their teachers have designed with and for them, such as feelings charades and practicing "I statements" in managing their emotions in relationships with others. They "give peace," quiet love with wiggling fingers and outstretched hands, and "appreciations." They participate in peace puppet roleplaying to imaginatively problem-pose and problem-solve together creative responses and possibilities for peace from real lived classroom conflicts.

Fourth-graders come together to seek to understand the violence in their own neighborhoods; and endorse voice, interest, inquiry, reflection, conversation, collaboration, and action as avenues of heart, hope, generosity, solidarity, empowerment, and transformation for peace. "When the integrative power of nonviolence plays out in multiple dimensions of education, differences do not lead to violence but to expansion of horizons for students to adopt new lenses, form new relationality, and acquire new knowledge" (Wang, in press, p. 12). What education explicitly pursues in terms of the mind, and knowledge, in this way also requires integrating and unifying efforts, apprehensions of the interconnectedness of all life and learning, cohering forces that make for genuine meaning at the heart of understanding—and such, impacting personhood, heart as well as mind, at the site of subjectivity and its sociality as well.

A Matter of the Heart: On Peace, Love, and Understanding

While—particularly with the pre-service teachers—in this study an emphasis on the import of the mind and consciousness was forwarded concerning the experience and pursuit of peace both personally and pedagogically, the heart was ever present with such as well— peace, this experience of "withness" engaging heart and mind as one. Here, too, peace not only involves a state of mind—intentional, and affiliated with knowledge, thought, and understanding, but also a heart space or emotional state—optimal, desirable, and affiliated with joy, happiness, pleasure, and love. Included herein, as well, is this ethics of responsibility, a sense of one's relationship to, identification with, and compassion and care for others, and the world in which one lives and is a part. The heart is "all in" herein.

Even as much is made of the mind and cultivating its powers, then, in education, of one sort or another—education, a human project for humans as *rational* or at least *thinking* animals; the heart, and its powers, are all too often forgotten or dismissed as "soft" or "irrational." Such relates to the abiding legacy of patriarchy (and ethnocentrism and colonialism), reason aligned with the privileged masculine, emotion with the subjugated feminine, and that of a worldview constituted by a profound dualism in the West, as has been mentioned, separating and alienating mind from heart, and/or body—and positivism, marking objectivity over and apart from subjectivity; making all matter, all that matters, material. This negligence, aside from research findings already cited above concerning goals, heart, and happiness, has proven to be somewhat persistently recalcitrant, however, especially in education, enamored as it is with "hard" numbers as the measure of all matters of import. Yet, we might consider that, according to the Institute of HeartMath Research Center, the measure of the heart matters much:

> The human heart emits the strongest electromagnetic field in our body. The heart's electromagnetic field is five thousand times stronger than the brain's electromagnetic field. This electromagnetic field envelops the entire body extending out in all directions, and it can be measured up to several feet outside of the body. Research shows that as we consciously focus on feeling a positive emotion it has a beneficial effect on our own health and well-being, and can have a positive effect on those around us. (Socialconsciousness.com, 2012)

And Western educational tradition, in many cases however paradoxically or amid contradictory claims, also surprisingly bears witness to the power and import of the heart, and of attending to such in education. For example, from Aristotle we are told: "Educating the mind without educating the heart is no education at all" (cited in Chang, Simon & Dong, 2012, p. 278). Most of us have heard Pascal's famous adage: "The heart has its reasons of which reason knows nothing" (cited in Fisher, 1987, p. 56). Philosophy, itself, something of the mother (or father) of all academic disciplines, denotes the *love* of wisdom. Of course, a favorite more contemporary word herein, and one that brings us back to peace directly, comes from Jimi Hendrix: "When the power of love overcomes the love of power, the world will know peace" (cited in Darder, 2012, p. xviii).

While respecting schools, there may be a great deal of focus, especially in the elementary years, on community building or student interest and motivation—the import and role of such—this work is albeit often engaged dominantly as a tool for classroom management (then, too, as a source of power over students and studies for teachers). While some attention is also given to cultivating particular dispositions and attitudes, or emotional intelligence (for example, Goleman, 1995) and socioemotional growth, much of it gets framed nearly wholly similarly by the managerial interests and cognitive aims of the educational institution, as well. Perhaps we still do not believe in the power of love, enamored by the love of power—and yet teaching teachers and students the same.

The children in this study spoke much, concerning learning and living peace, of that which engages the heart, and of the power of such: for good—as in being recognized, listened to, respected, and cared for, and giving the same to others; as having fun with friends at school rather than boredom or diminishment; as finding what one loves and being able to engage and grow in and share such with others. Yet, much too was spoken of this power for ill: when the heart is tied up in dark feelings, difficult conflicts, or unacknowledged, incapacitated, abandoned. The sobering sense with which my time with these elementary students left me was that while they aspired to peace, they still knew violence to be a stronger and more effectual force in their lives and in the world. What if we pedagogically, in the cause of peace, and humanity, explicitly and actively, and foundationally, took up the work of the heart, and heart-work—teachers and students teaching, learning, studying, living together the power of love, and engaging in practicing practices of love (inclusive of self, others, ideas, the world, etc., through multiple cultural, epistemological, wisdom traditions, and manifold relationships with others)?

Peace, Pedagogy and the World:
The Responsibility of Being Fully Human

In Fromm's (1956/2006) analysis, he claims that: "love is an action, the practice of a human power, which can be practiced only in freedom and never as the result of a compulsion" (p. 21); in this act "lies the expression of my [one's] aliveness" (p. 22), which is "the highest expression of potency" (p. 21). Concerning the experience of this power, he speaks of the child who at last realizes he or she can not only gladly receive, but also make for and give something to mother or father, attend to needs, express care, share of himself or herself—even the most precious gift, what is alive within—in a way that enhances not only mother or father but self as well. It is in genuine, active, "productive" (in the sense that something new is born for and between, in this case, parent and child) relation to and with each other, then, that we come to know and live, teach and learn, the power of love, and the power of peace as well. And such, ever, is enacted in the here and now, moment-by-moment, at the site of our subjectivity, and "situation," in the body, with others, in the real and lived world in which we dwell.

While it is difficult, if not impossible, to truly conclude in any considerations of peace and the pursuit of peace, and such pedagogically, in this moment, via these inquiries and engagements with aspiring and practicing teachers, and some of their elementary classrooms and students, such contemplations have culminated for me in a heightened attention to our relationships—and to their transformation and power, particularly via love therein as power: those with self, other(s), and with and in the world we share. Attuning ourselves to peace in such—via mind and heart—ultimately also requires engagement of body, enacting, acting, and actualizing peace dreams in our daily lives and living. We not only purposely ponder and promote passion for, but also practice peace, and practice practicing peace—peace praxes in action, in cultivating our personhood. Such returns us to Arendt (1954/1993) with whom I also began this work, who postulates education as existing solely because new beings come into the world—others, distinctly singular, and distinctly distinct from generations before—for and to whom we are responsible, and they to and for us as well. This responsibility, too, involves the call of the world that is our home, especially in that its renewal, and ours, are together mutually bound. Education, in this, implicitly then, involves something of the work of peace—affirming life—the unity of life, harmonizing relations, and all for *amor mundi*—in love to and for the world, and its continuation, which is also the continuation of human life therein.

One of Arendt's mentors, Heidegger (1927/1962)—who writes much of the being that is human, as being-with-others, and being-in-the-world—defines human being via the German term *Dasein*, meaning literally there-being or being-there. The notion he seeks here to convey, at least in part, is that the being that is human is ever and always constituted by its "there." This peace we would be, become, teach, and reach, is thus ever aspired to and achieved in the body, as we live and breathe and have our being in the world, with others. In this way, it is not insignificant that both aspiring and practicing teachers and students in this study depicted peace as experienced in large measure via images of nature and art and playful activity. Such portraits point to the affirmation of our relationship to life beyond ourselves—and than even the simply human, to a world larger than ourselves, of which we are a part and which addresses us, blesses us, and calls for our genuine response; as well as to the understanding, joy, and freedom to be realized in fully engaging in life with others, via the senses—sens-uously experienced experience and expressive-ness.

As curriculum theorist and dancer Donald Blumenfeld-Jones (2012) argues, aesthetics, the body, agency, and ethics are integrally related in this way. Alas, such have also been in effect educationally undermined; given our enduring cultural dualism, and its patriarchal and imperial contours, which privileges separation—the mind over, against, and at detriment to the body. Certainly at odds with peace, and productive of manifold forms of violence, this frame contributes to the devaluation, domination, and degradation of: emotion, the female/feminine, and the earth; experience and knowledge gleaned via the senses, and thus also nature, aesthetics and play; and knowledge systems, peoples and cultures—all—designated as "oth-er," outside and apart from this objectified hierarchy of dualistic rationality. This recognition relates directly, too, to the insights of participants in this study, and recommendations in much of the peace education literature (for example, Bajaj & Brantmeier, 2011; Chubbuck and Zembylas, 2011; and Carr & Porfilio, 2012) as well, concerning the need to address inequitable power relations, and the suffering and social problems issuing from them—for example, those involving gender, class, race, ecology, such as rape, homelessness, racial vio-lence, addiction, and pollution, among much more besides. For many, pedagogically, this work involves not only cultivating critical aware-ness of such injustice, but also giving students the skills and tools required to resolve conflict and build peace and creating avenues for agency and action in seeking to eradicate inequity in promoting social justice.

Additionally, participants in this study endorsed, in this way, ac-tively disrupting the status quo in teaching and learning, introducing marginalized and diverse and conflicting perspectives via the curriculum. They advocated responsive, student-centered anti-oppressive pedagogy; culturally rich, relevant, and sensitive curriculum; and projects rooted in authentic collaborative inquiry, problem posing, service learning, and social action. Efforts to challenge traditional classroom hierarchies, too, toward some forms of shared governance and equality of relations, were seen in the first grade with its peace corner used by children at their discretion and of their choosing, its community promises collectively negotiated and agreed to, and its peace patrol wherein children helped each other resolve conflicts as they arose.

The fourth-graders' collaboratively designed their inquiry curriculum around a community problem they shared, one in which too they explicitly explored and sought to address unjust power relations, particularly respecting race, class, and gender. Some participants advised inquiry and action projects such as relating to racism, homophobia, bullying, littering, environmental degradation, and vandalism as well. In honing in also on providing students with the tools and skills needed to respond to violence as well as seek to make peace, aspiring teachers and practicing teachers acknowledged and asserted the call, on the part of both teachers and students, to struggle and labor, singularly and together, in taking up the responsibility, in participatory citizenship, to cultivate peace. As Wang, so viscerally puts it, such action "takes nothing less than nonviolence to work *through* the knot of violence" (Wang, in press, p. 4).

Yet, in such, we do well to remind ourselves not to fall merely to the instrumental herein, implementing programs for social action and justice; for peace—and as the presence itself of justice (King, cited in Carson, 2000, p. 170)—requires the art of love, including the play of freedom and experience of wholeness and meaning therein. Thus, herein too are implications for the work and way of peace concerning the import of the arts, of the aesthetic, and of play—embodying justice and peace in and through the beauty of lived and dynamic and spontaneous encounters, explorations, and relations. Emersion in such not only, as a matter of pedagogy, allows for students to freely engage with a diversity of discourses, modes of understanding, forms of inquiry, materials and mediums, and avenues for expression, but also makes for new and many connections, empowering growth and creativity, as well as for experiencing the world aesthetically. Blumen-feld-Jones (2012) discusses what I am suggesting needs to become, for peace, also a priority to cultivate through curriculum and pedagogy, in ourselves, in teachers, and in students:

> Living aesthetically...an active participation in the world through one's senses, the outcome of such engagement being unknowable before-hand...but having a profound effect on one's sense of place and value in the world.... It is...connected to living life in relation to others such that...we come to a realization of our responsibility for others, not through learning that we have responsibilities but through actively sensing the other as need-ing us. (pp. 30, 21)

Embracing the aesthetic, as opposed to flattening human experi-ence and knowledge as happens so much in education as presently undertaken, rather heightens our sensitivity to and apprehension of such—embodied, too, as this embrace is, as is also the art of play, its kindred. Yet presently, we suffer and have brought upon children, and this also via education, what has actually been called "nature deficit disorder" (for example, Louv, 2008), in which also a "play crisis" (for example, O'Brien & Smith, 2002; Elkind, 2007; Gray, 2011) has been declared and is of growing concern. Educators, psycholo-gists, and others who work with children have even begun to gather to address this concern, considered by some to be a new civil rights issue, as well.[11] Yet, in schools, in the name of excellence in educa-tion, we eliminate recesses, replace free play and conversation with direct and scripted instruction, and increasingly exert control over and stifle the movement of the young bodies of growing, active, and curious children—and this, despite even overwhelming evidence of the cognitive/intellectual/academic benefits of play.

Of course, photographs of peace and discussions of peace by par-ticipants in this study are deeply rooted in the experiences of play, beauty, wonder, and celebration. Peace places are filled with visions

---

11 In Philadelphia, September 20–22, 2013, for example, interested educators, psychologists, and others gathered at the "Declaration of Play" Conference to explore possibilities for reclaiming childhood and the future in affirming play as a responsi-bility and right.

of peace—symbols, memorials, icons, inspirations, as well as music, laughter, humor, art, and nature's bounty. If we consider the heart of nonviolence from so many wisdom traditions (for example, Buddhism, Hinduism, Jainism) in *ahimsa*, signifying "no harm," and also a way of living that acknowledges the magic, mystery, and sacredness of all life, such also communicates an affirmation of the life of the body and an affinity with all life, and advocates friendship with such too. And where can friendship begin, exist, or grow without beauty and wonder and play? What if, aiming for peace to cultivate a reverence and respect for all life, and treasured relations of friendship, we truly took up the work of education, designed curriculum and pedagogy, with aesthetic living in mind? Rich exposure to and engagement with nature, and with play, among our core curriculum standards? Playing and paying peace forward in freedom, joy, and generosity?

Reimaging Peace, and Pedagogically: "Whole, Bright, Deep with Understanding"

In a piece endorsing qualitative research as "politically progressive" and "epistemologically sophisticated" in its understanding that the meaning of human life involves movement, conflict, and resolution, the relationships among which press toward giving "birth to a new order of understanding and life," Pinar (1988, p. 151) urges us to contribute to such labor, in work with ourselves as well as work with others in the world. Elucidating the role specifically autobiography— and thus subjectivity—plays in such labor, he draws upon a character in Virginia Woolf's *The Years* (1937, pp. 427–428, cited in Pinar, 1988, p. 151), in likening it to blow-up photography, and in seeking to describe what such magnifies and makes visible:

> We know nothing, even about ourselves. We're only just beginning, she thought, to understand, here and there. She held her hand hallowed; she felt she wanted to enclose the present and future, until it shone, whole, bright, deep with understanding.

I hope I, too, have held my hand hallowed, in seeking to picture peace, and here and there possibilities for peace and pedagogies of and for peace among us, with these generous pre-service and practicing teachers and elementary students with whom I have thought— and before my readers. I hope the call to engage afresh *the peace that passeth understanding, the peace that bringeth understanding, "the understanding that bringeth peace"* (Keller, cited in Lichtenstein, 1962)—in purpose and passion and praxis, has indeed shone whole and deep and bright, as well: a call held dear by all, enclosed in many hallowed hands. For, we have only, truly, just begun. *Beginning with me, beginning with you, beginning with us; imagine all the people, together… Imagine.*

Bibliography

Aoki, T. (2005). *Education in a new key: The collected works of Ted T. Aoki* (W. Pinar, ed.). Mahweh, NJ: Lawrence Erlbaum.

Apple, M. (2004). *Ideology and curriculum.* (3rd ed.). New York, NY: Routledge.

Apple, M. (2006). *Educating the "right" way: Markets, standards, God and inequality* (2nd ed.). New York, NY: Routledge.

Arendt, H. (1954/1993). *Between past and future* (D. Lindley, trans.). New York, NY: Penguin Books.

Arendt, H. (2006). *Eichmann in Jerusalem: A report on the banality of evil.* New York, NY: Penguin.

Asher, N. (2009, March). Writing home/decolonizing text(s). Discourse, *30*(1), 1–13.

Aurobindo, S. (1993). *The integral yoga: Sri Aurobindo's teaching and method of practice.* Pondicherry, India: Sri Aurobindo Ashram Trust.

Bajaj, M. (2008). "Critical" peace education. *Encyclopedia of peace education*(pp. 135–146). Charlotte, NC: Information Age Publishing.

Bajaj, M., & Brantmeier, E. (2011, November). The politics, praxis, and possibilities of critical peace education. *Journal of Peace Education, 8*(3), 221–224.

Bernard, J. (2013, October 1). *The gift of goals.* Lecture conducted as part of Women's Week (Women's Council of Greater Baton Rouge), Baton Rouge, LA.

Beuchner, F. (1991). *Now and then: A memoir of vocation.* San Francisco, CA: HarperCollins.

Biedermann, H. (1994). *Dictionary of symbols: Cultural icons and the meanings behind them* (J. Hulbert, trans.). New York, NY: Meridian.

Biesta, G. (2010). A new logic of emancipation: The methodology of Jacques Ranciere. *Educational Theory, 60*(1), 39–59.

Blumenfeld-Jones, D. (2012). *Curriculum and the aesthetic life: Hermeneutics, body, democracy, and ethics in curriculum theory and practice.* New York, NY: Peter Lang.

Bowen-Moore, P. (1989). *Hannah Arendt's philosophy of natality.* New York, NY: St. Martin's Press.

Cameron, J. (1992). *The artist's way: A spiritual path of higher creativity.* New York, NY: G. P. Putnam's Sons.

Carr, P., & Porfilio, B. (Eds.). (2012). *Educating for peace in a time of permanent war: Are schools part of the solution or the problem?* New York, NY: Routledge.

Carson, C. (Ed.). (2000). *The papers of Martin Luther King, Jr., Volume IV:Symbol of the movement, January 1957–December 1958.* Berkeley, CA: University of California Press.

Chang, E. S., Simon, M., & Dong, X. (2012). Integrating cultural humility into health care professional education and training. *Advances in Health Sciences Education, 17*(2), 269–278.

Chubbuck, S. M., & Zembylas, M. (2011, November). Toward a critical pedagogy for nonviolence in urban school contexts. *Journal of Peace Education, 8*(3), 259–275.

Coerr, E. (1979). *Sadako and the thousand paper cranes.* New York, NY: BDD Books.

Cousins, N. (1956). We will not have peace by afterthought. *Saturday Review.*

Cowhey, M. (2006). *Black ants and Buddhists: Thinking critically and teaching differently in the primary grades.* Portland, ME: Stenhouse.

Critchley, S., & Kearney, R. (1997/2006). Preface. In J. Derrida, *On cosmopolitanism and forgiveness* (p. vii–xii) (M. Dooley & M. Hughes, trans.). New York, NY: Routledge.

Csikszentmihalyi, M. (1990). *Flow: The psychology of optimal experience.* New York, NY: Harper & Row.

Dalai Lama. (1999). Education and the human heart. In S. Glazer (Ed.), *The heart of learning* (pp. 85–96). New York, NY: Penguin.

Dalai Lama. (2007, October). *Peace and prosperity.* Public lecture presented at Radio City Music Hall, New York City.

Darder, A. (2012). In search of peace in a culture of war. In P. Carr & B. Porfilio (Eds.), *Educating for peace in a time of permanent war: Are schools part of the solution or the problem?* New York, NY: Routledge.

Davies, B. (2006). Subjectification: The relevance of Butler's analysis for education. *British Journal of Sociology of Education, 27*(4), 425–438.

Delpit, L. (2006). *Other people's children: Cultural conflict in the classroom.* New York, NY: The New Press.

den Heyer, K. (2009). What if curriculum (of a certain sort) doesn't matter? *Curriculum Inquiry, 39*(1), 27–40.

Derrida, J. (1985). *The ear of the other: Otobiography, transference, translation.* New York, NY: Schocken Books.

Dewey, J. (1916). *Democracy and education.* New York, NY: Free Press.

Dewey, J. (1938). *Experience and education.* New York, NY: Macmillan.

Dewey, J. (1957). *Human nature and conduct: An introduction to social psychology.* New York, NY: Modern Library.

Doll, W., Jr. (1993). *A postmodern perspective on curriculum.* New York, NY: Teachers College Press.

Donoghue, D. (1984). *Connoisseurs of chaos: Ideas of order in modern American poetry.* New York, NY: Columbia University Press.

Eisner, E. (1979/2001). *The educational imagination: On the design and evaluation of school programs* (3rd ed.). New York, NY: Macmillan.

Elkind, D. (2007). *The power of play: Learning what comes naturally.* Philadelphia, PA: Perseus Books.

Fish, S. (2007, April). Save the world on your own time: What professors should not do. Lecture presented at Teachers College, Columbia University, New York.

Fish, S. (2008). *Save the world on your own time.* Oxford, UK: Oxford University Press.

Fisher, B. (1987). The heart has its reasons: Feeling, thinking, and community-building in feminist education. *Women's Studies Quarterly, 15*(3/4), 47–58.

Fontana, D. (1993). *The secret language of symbols: A visual key to symbols and their meanings.* San Francisco, CA: Chronicle.

Forencich, F. (2009). *Exuberant animal: The power of health, play and joyful movement.* Bloomington, IN: Author House.

Frankl, V. (1946/1997). *Man's search for meaning.* New York: Simon & Schuster.

Freire, P. (1970/1993). *Pedagogy of the oppressed* (M. Ramos, trans.). New York, NY: Continuum.

Fromm, E. (1956/2006). *The art of loving.* New York, NY: HarperCollins.

Galtung, J. (1990). Cultural violence. *Journal of Peace Research, 6*(3), 167–191.

Gandhi. (1958). *Collected works.* Delhi, India: Publications Division, Ministry of Information and Broadcasting, Government of India.

Garrison, J. (2011). Compassionate, spiritual, and creative listening in teaching and learning. *Teachers College Record, 112*(11), 4–5.

Gaudelli, W. (2011). Global seeing. *Teachers College Record, 113*(6), 7–8.

Gemstone Peace Education Team. (2008). Peace education aimed at children everywhere in the world. In J. Lin, E. Brantmeier, & C. Bruhn (Eds.), *Transforming education for peace* (pp. 93–111). Charlotte, NC: Information Age Publishing.

Genor, M., & Goodwin, A. L. (2005). Confronting ourselves: Using autobiographical analysis in teacher education. *The New Educator, 1*(4), 311–331.

Gray, P. (2011). The decline of play and the rise of psychopathology in children and adolescents. *American Journal of Play, 3*(4), 443–463.

Greene, M. (2008, March). *The poet, the city and curriculum.* Paper presented at the American Association for the Advancement of Curriculum Studies (AAACS) Conference, New York.

Gunaratnam, Y. (2007, November). Where is the love? Art, aesthetics and research. *Journal of Social Work Practice, 21*(3), 271–287.

Hanh, T. N. (1987/1996). *Being peace.* Berkeley, CA: Parallax Press.

Hanh, T. N. (1992). *Peace is every step: The path of mindfulness in everyday life.* New York, NY: Bantam Books.

Hanh, T. N. (1999). *Going home: Jesus and Buddha as brothers.* New York: Riverhead Press.

Hansen, D. (2008). Curriculum and the idea of a cosmopolitan inheritance. *Journal of Curriculum Studies, 40*(3), 289–312.

Hansen, D. (2011). Introduction: Rethinking globalization, education, citizenship. *Teachers College Record, 113*(6), 1–2.

Hantzopoulos, M. (2011, November). Institutionalizing critical peace education in public schools: A case for comprehensive implementation. *Journal of Peace Education, 8*(3), 225–242.

Heidegger, M. (1927/1962). *Being and time.* (J. Macquarrie & E. Robinson, trans.). San Francisco, CA: Harper & Row.

Hershock, P. (2009). Ethics in an era of reflexive modernization. In J. Powers & C. Prebish (Eds.), *Destroying Mara forever* (pp. 151–164). Ithaca, NY: Snow Lion.

Hope, J. (1997). *The secret language of the soul: A visual guide to the spiritual world.* San Francisco, CA: Chronicle.

Horowitz, D. (2009, April). *One-party classroom: How radical professors at America's top colleges indoctrinate students and undermine our democracy.* Lecture presented at Teachers College, Columbia University, New York.

Horowitz, D. (2009). *One-party classroom: How radical professors at America's top colleges indoctrinate students and undermine democracy.* New York, NY: Crown Forum.

Huebner, D. (1999). *The lure of the transcendent: Collected essays by Dwayne E. Huebner.* Mahwah, NJ: Lawrence Erlbaum Associates.

Jackson, P. (1968/1990). *Life in classrooms.* New York, NY: Teachers College Press.

Kincheloe, J. (2002). *The sign of the burger: McDonald's and the culture of power.* Philadelphia, PA: Temple University Press.

Kincheloe, J. (2004). *Critical pedagogy.* New York, NY: Peter Lang.

Kolsbun, K., & Sweeney, M. (2008). *Peace: The biography of a symbol.* New York, NY: National Geographic.

Krishnamurti, J. (1996). *Total freedom: The essential Krishnamurti.* Ojai, CA: Krishnamurti Foundation Trust.

Ladson-Billings, G. (2009). *The dreamkeepers: Successful teachers of African-American children.* San Francisco, CA: John Wiley & Sons.

Lantieri, L. (Ed.). (2002). *Schools with spirit: Nurturing the inner lives of children and teachers.* New York, NY: Beacon Press.

Lather, P. (2007) *Getting lost: Feminist efforts toward a double(d) science*. Albany, NY: SUNY Press.

Lennon, J. (1971). Imagine. On *Imagine* [record]. London, UK: Apple Records.

Lesser, R. (1984). *Hansel and Gretel* (illus. by Zelinsky, P.). New York, NY: Puffin Books.

Lichtenstein, A. (1962). *Henry More: The rational theology of a Cambridge Platonist*. Cambridge, MA: Harvard University Press.

Linstroth, J. P. (2005, Fall). An introductory essay: Are we in "the Age of Resistance" in a post-9/11 world? *Conflict and Peace Studies*, 12(2), 1–21.

Loewen, J. W. (2007). *Lies my teacher told me: Everything your American history textbook got wrong*. New York, NY: Simon & Schuster.

Louv, R. (2008). *Last child in the woods: Saving our children from nature deficit disorder*. New York, NY: Workman.

Macdonald, J. (1995). A transcendental-developmental ideology of education. In B. J. Macdonald (Ed.), *Theory as a prayerful act: The collected essays of James B. Macdonald* (pp. 69–98). New York, NY: Peter Lang.

Macer, D. R. J., & Saad-Zoy, S. (Eds.). (2010). *Asian-Arab philosophical dialogues on war and peace*. Bangkok, TH: UNESCO Bangkok.

McCarthy, C. (Ed.). (2001). *Strength through peace*. Washington, DC: Center for Teaching Peace.

McGinn, N. (1996). Education, democratization, and globalization: A challenge for comparative education. *Comparative Education Review*, 40(4), 341–357.

McGlynn, Jackie. (2011). *I am...in the garden*. Bloomington, IN: WestBow Press.

Mehrotra, R. (2005).*The essential Dalai Lama: His important teachings*. New York, NY: Penguin.

Myss, C. (2004). *Acts of power: Channeling grace in your everyday life*. New York, NY: Free Press.

Navarro-Castro, L., & Nario-Galace, J. (2008). *Peace education: A pathway to a culture of peace*. San Francisco, CA: Scribe.

Noddings, N. (2005). *The challenge to care in schools: An alternative approach to education* (2nd ed.). New York: Teachers College Press.

Norris, K. (1931). *The sacrifice years*. New York, NY: P Group, Inc.

Nussbaum, M. (1997). *Cultivating humanity: A classical defense of reform in liberal education*. Cambridge, MA: Harvard University Press.

Obama, B. (2012, December 14). President Obama makes a statement about the shooting in Newtown, Connecticut. Retrieved fromhttp://www.whitehouse.gov

O'Brien, J., & Smith, J. (2002). Childhood transformed? Risk perceptions and the decline of free play. *British Journal of Occupational Therapy, 65*(3), 123–128.

Pailliotet, A. (1998). Deep viewing: A critical look at visual texts. In J. Kincheloe & S. Steinberg (Eds.), *Unauthorized methods: Strategies for critical teaching* (pp. 123–151). New York, NY: Routledge.

Pedersen, P. (2007). *Counseling across cultures.* Thousand Oaks, CA: Sage.

Pinar, W. (1988). "Whole, bright, deep with understanding": Issues in qualitative research and autobiographical method. In W. Pinar (Ed.), *Contemporary curriculum discourses* (pp. 134–153). Scottsdale, AZ: Gorsuch Scarisbrick.

Pinar, W. (2004). *What is curriculum theory?* Mahwah, NJ: Lawrence Erlbaum Associates.

Pinar, W. (2009). *The worldliness of a cosmopolitan education: Passionate lives in public service.* New York, NY: Routledge.

Pinar, W. (2012). *What is curriculum theory?* (2nd ed.). Mahweh, NJ: Lawrence Erlbaum.

Plato. (ca. 380 BC/1992). *Republic.* (G.M.A. Grube, trans.). Indianapolis, IN: Hackett.

Pope John Paul II. (1979, January 1). *Message of His Holiness Pope John Paul II for the celebration of the Day of Peace.* Retrieved from http://www.vatican.va/

Poplin, M. (1999, Fall). The global classroom of the 21st century: Lessons from Mother Teresa and imperatives from Columbine. *Educational Horizons, 78*(1), 30–38.

Puigvert, L. (2010, November). *Findings from CREA's Women and Violence Study.* Paper presented at the Paulo and Nita Freire International Critical Pedagogy Project Conference, Granada, Spain.

Quinn, M. (2001). *Going out, not knowing whither: Education, the upward journey and the faith of reason.* New York, NY: Peter Lang.

Quinn, M. (2009). "No room in the inn"? The question of hospitality in the post(partum)-labors of curriculum studies. In E. Malewski (Ed.), *A curriculum handbook: The next moment.* New York: Routledge.

Quinn, M. (2010). 'Ex and the city': On cosmopolitanism, community and the 'curriculum of refuge.' *Transnational Curriculum Inquiry, 7*(1), 77–102.

Quinn, M. (2011). On natality in our roots, routes, and relations: Reconceiving the "3 R's" at the rendezvous of education, citizenship, and globalization. *Teachers College Record, 113*(6), 6–7.

Quinn, M., Moon, S., Roth, M., Roepke, T., Suh, Y., Sonu, D., & Egan-Cunningham, K. (2013). The eye/I of justice in "currere": A readers theater performance and curriculum conversation. Manuscript in preparation.

Ranciere, J. (1991). *The ignorant schoolmaster: Five lessons in intellectual emancipation.* (K. Ross, trans.). Stanford, CA: Stanford University Press.

Reardon, B. (2000). *Peace education: A review and projection.* In B. Moon, S. Brown, & M. Ben Peretz (Eds.), *Routledge international companion to education* (pp. 397–425). New York: Routledge.

Reardon, B. (2013). Mediating on the barricades: Concerns, cautions, and possibilities for peace education for political efficacy. In P. Trifonas & B. Wright (Eds.), *Critical peace education: Difficult dialogues* (pp. 1–28). New York: Springer.

Reardon, B., & Snauwaert, D. (2011). Reflective pedagogy, cosmopolitanism, and critical peace education for political efficacy: A discussion of Betty A. Reardon's assessment of the field. *In Factis Pax: In Knowledge {There is}Peace, 5*(1), 1–14.

Ricoeur, P. (1995/2000). *The just* (D. Pallauer, trans.). Chicago, IL: University of Chicago Press.

Scheurich, J. (1997/2001). *Research method in the postmodern.* London, UK: Routledge Falmer.

Schlup, L., & Whisenhunt, D. (2001). *It seems to me: Selected letters of Eleanor Roosevelt.* Lexington: University Press of Kentucky.

Shi, J./Leong, L. (in progress). *Returning the light to shine within: A Buddhist moral democratic currere in third space.* Unpublished manuscript.

Sleeter, C. (2005).*Un-standardizing curriculum: Multicultural teaching in the standards-based classroom.* New York: Teachers College Press.

Social-consciousness.com. (2012, December 24). The intelligent heart: Institute of HeartMath. Retrieved from http://www.social-consciousness.com/2012/12/science-of-heart-institute-of-heartmath.html

Sonu, D. (2013). In the pursuit of peace: A qualitative study on classroom co-existence and subjectification in four elementary school classrooms. Unpublished manuscript.

Stockland, P. (2008). *The assassination of John F. Kennedy.* Edina, MN: ABDO.

Stowers, C. (1998). *To the last breath: Three women fight for the truth behind a child's tragic murder.* New York: St. Martin's Press.

Taubman, P. (2009) *Teaching by numbers: Deconstructing the discourse of standards and accountability in education.* New York: Routledge.

Trifonas, P., & Wright, B. (Eds.). (2013). *Critical peace education: Difficult dialogues.* New York: Springer.

Tutu, N. (2013, September, 27). *Ubuntu: The challenge of being human.* Lecture conducted as part of Women's Week (Women's Council of Greater Baton Rouge), Baton Rouge, LA.

Wang, H. (2010). A zero space of nonviolence. *Journal of Curriculum Theorizing, 26*(1), 1–8.

Wang, H. (in press). A nonviolent perspective on internationalizing curriculum studies. In W. Pinar (Ed.), *International handbook of curriculum research* (2nd ed.). Mahwah, NJ: Lawrence Erlbaum.

Werner, W. (2004). "What does this picture say?" Reading the intertextuality of visual images. *International Journal of Social Education, 19*(1), 64–82.

Westbrook, R. (1991). *John Dewey and American democracy.* Ithaca, NY: Cornell University Press.

Wexler, P. (1992). *Becoming somebody: Toward a social psychology of school.* Abington, Oxon: RoutledgeFalmer.

Wexler, P. (2000). *The mystical society: An emerging social vision.* Boulder, CO: Westview Press.

Wexler, P. (2002). Chaos and cosmos: Educational discourse and social change. *Journal of Curriculum Studies, 34*(4), 469–479.

Wilder, T. (2007). *Thornton Wilder: Collected plays and writings on theater* (J. D. McCarthy, ed.). New York, NY: Penguin.

Wolf, N. (2007). *The end of America: Letter of warning to a young patriot.* White River Junction, VT: Chelsea Green.

Woolf, V. (1937). *The years.* New York, NY: Harcourt, Brace.

Index

in Education

Peter Lang Primers are designed to provide a brief and concise introduction or supplement to specific topics in education. Although sophisticated in content, these primers are written in an accessible style, making them perfect for undergraduate and graduate classroom use. Each volume includes a glossary of key terms and a References and Resources section.

Other published and forthcoming volumes cover such topics as:

- Standards
- Popular Culture
- Critical Pedagogy
- Literacy
- Higher Education
- John Dewey
- Feminist Theory and Education

- Studying Urban Youth Culture
- Multiculturalism through Postformalism
- Creative Problem Solving
- Teaching the Holocaust
- Piaget and Education
- Deleuze and Education
- Foucault and Education

Look for more Peter Lang Primers to be published soon. To order other volumes, please contact our Customer Service Department:
     800-770-LANG (within the US)
     212-647-7706 (outside the US)
     212-647-7707 (fax)

To find out more about this and other Peter Lang book series, or to browse a full list of education titles, please visit our website:
     www.peterlang.com